DI017549

# POWER OF THE BEST

ALSO BY JOHN HUGHES

*Building the Best:*
*Lessons from Inside Canada's Best Managed Companies*
by John Hughes
(and Anthony Grnak and Douglas Hunter)

# POWER OF THE BEST

Innovative Strategies from Canada's Best Managed Companies

## Peter Brown and John Hughes

PORTFOLIO
PENGUIN

PORTFOLIO PENGUIN
an imprint of Penguin Canada

Published by the Penguin Group
Penguin Group (Canada), 90 Eglinton Avenue East, Suite 700, Toronto, Ontario, Canada M4P 2Y3

Penguin Group (USA) Inc., 375 Hudson Street, New York, New York 10014, U.S.A.
Penguin Books Ltd, 80 Strand, London WC2R 0RL, England
Penguin Ireland, 25 St Stephen's Green, Dublin 2, Ireland (a division of Penguin Books Ltd)
Penguin Group (Australia), 250 Camberwell Road, Camberwell, Victoria 3124, Australia
  (a division of Pearson Australia Group Pty Ltd)
Penguin Books India Pvt Ltd, 11 Community Centre, Panchsheel Park, New Delhi – 110 017, India
Penguin Group (NZ), 67 Apollo Drive, Rosedale, Auckland 0632, New Zealand
  (a division of Pearson New Zealand Ltd)
Penguin Books (South Africa) (Pty) Ltd, 24 Sturdee Avenue, Rosebank, Johannesburg 2196,
  South Africa

Penguin Books Ltd, Registered Offices: 80 Strand, London WC2R 0RL, England

First published 2012

1 2 3 4 5 6 7 8 9 10  (FR)

Copyright © Deloitte & Touche LLP, 2012

All rights reserved. Without limiting the rights under copyright reserved above, no part of this
publication may be reproduced, stored in or introduced into a retrieval system, or transmitted in
any form or by any means (electronic, mechanical, photocopying, recording or otherwise), without
the prior written permission of both the copyright owner and the above publisher of this book.

Manufactured in Canada.

LIBRARY AND ARCHIVES CANADA CATALOGUING IN PUBLICATION

Brown, Peter Ernest
  Power of the best : innovative strategies from Canada's
  best managed companies / Peter Brown and John Hughes.

Includes index.

ISBN 978-0-670-06645-2

1. Industrial management—Canada—Case studies.  2. Business enterprises—Canada—Case studies.
3. Entrepreneurship—Canada—Case studies.  4. Success in business—Canada—Case studies.
I. Hughes, John, 1964–  II. Title.

HD38.25.C3B76 2012      658.400971      C2012-903988-8

Visit the Penguin Canada website at **www.penguin.ca**

Special and corporate bulk purchase rates available; please see
**www.penguin.ca/corporatesales** or call 1-800-810-3104, ext. 2477.

**ALWAYS LEARNING**                                          **PEARSON**

# CONTENTS

# PREFACE

When we began the journey of Canada's Best Managed Companies twenty years ago, our vision was to build the largest network of exceptional Canadian businesses so they could help one another succeed. We wanted to foster a community of owners, managers, and employees that would enrich lives as well as businesses. *The Power of the Best* captures much of this vision and celebrates the collective passion of individuals working together to build businesses that benefit the communities in which they operate and that leave valuable, lasting legacies in Canada.

Canada's Best Managed Companies program began in the recession of the early 1990s, when plant closings and job losses were the order of the day. The mainstream media focused on these unfortunate stories and overlooked the sea of small private companies that were finding ways to start and expand, creating employment for Canadians. One might think that a recession would not be the best time to launch a program to celebrate Canadian business, but it was actually the perfect time.

•  •  •

The way we evaluate the candidates for Canada's Best Managed Companies each year encourages leaders to articulate how they address key challenges. Those challenges fall into three broad categories: strategy, capability, and commitment.

When we consider a company's strategy we seek to answer two questions:

1. Where does the company want to play?
2. How do they win?

These questions are purposefully set so they produce the first answers that companies must articulate when applying for Canada's Best Managed Companies program. Companies must explain succinctly their unique offerings to the marketplace and how they build value. They are asked to provide an overview of their business model and planning process, and to show how these are adapted to the economic environment and communicated throughout the organization. Most important, in this section companies must clearly outline why their strategic plan is demonstrably superior to that of their competitors. We look at the key pieces of that strategy, including

- Core competencies
- Development of innovative, winning products and services
- Mergers, acquisitions, and alliances
- Going global
- Detailed sales and marketing plans
- Attention to corporate social responsibility

Having set the strategic table, companies move on to the next phase, to answer the question of how they will execute the strategy. This forces companies to think through how they develop the capabilities required to compete and how they deliver on their strategic intent. Here we ask companies to focus on three main capabilities and describe the process for accelerating their development in their organizations. Those capabilities are

1. Building and sustaining a customer focused approach to sales and marketing
2. Raising capital and managing finances
3. Capitalizing on the use of technologies and solutions

The most important aspect of this section of the submission is the way these capabilities link directly back to the strategic questions outlined in the first section. Without these links, the company and its management team risk not achieving their goals.

The third section of the questionnaire focuses on one of the most vital issues for any business: how it develops talent and leaders, which is among the most crucial challenges in building a sustainable and valuable company. Critical to the success of any organization is management's ability to lead by communicating its vision throughout the organization, and attracting and retaining the talent necessary to build a culture that supports the strategy, capabilities, and vision of the company. We ask a company to look at its long-term business plan and explain what it is doing today to build the next group of leaders. Again, we require companies to demonstrate how their strategies and best practices for engaging and retaining employees and building a supportive culture tie directly back to the capabilities required to achieve the strategic objectives outlined in the first section.

The integration of these three cornerstones of the business—strategy, capability, commitment—differentiate Best Managed

Companies from their competitors. Our experience has shown that Best Managed Companies are adept at integrating these cornerstones and ensuring that they work together to build a solid foundation for success.

The review of the cornerstones of capability and commitment has been a positive experience not only for the companies that have gone on to be recognized as Canada's Best Managed Companies. We have found that over the course of interviews at thousands of companies during the last twenty years, many of them benefit from the insights gained in applying this review process to their businesses. In fact, many of these companies have incorporated these insights into their strategic planning and business processes. This has helped us to achieve our vision of benefitting all Canadian companies through their association with the program.

●  ●  ●

As we celebrate our program's twentieth anniversary, we are often asked two questions: What has changed the most over those twenty years with regard to the Best Managed Companies? And, more important, what has stayed the same? In describing what has stayed the same, two key aspects of Canadian entrepreneurs and their businesses have stood out. One is the ability of Best Managed Companies to adapt to the rapidly changing business environment. Adaptability is a necessary skill, particularly in the current climate with its accelerated pace of change driven by technological advances and business globalization. The other enduring characteristic of Canadian business is sustainability. As you will read in the coming chapters, Best Managed Companies in Canada are always looking to build sustainable platforms. Given their modest size relative to global competitors and with limited financial resources, these businesses have plans that are well thought out, controlled investments that, like all efficient deployments of capital, are seeking the highest rate of return.

While our first book, *Building the Best*, focused on growth challenges and strategy, capability and commitment, *Power of the Best* deals specifically with key themes we have seen over the past twenty years. It provides a retrospective of the rich history of each profiled company, touching on the strategic milestones in the life of the business and, most important, the stories told by family members.

*Power of the Best* is a book for owners and entrepreneurs, for management and employees, for students of business and those who have an interest in business. It is a book for all Canadians, with business success stories all Canadians should be proud of.

# INTRODUCTION

## A HISTORY OF ENTREPRENEURSHIP: CANADA'S BEST MANAGED COMPANIES PROGRAM

Established in 1993, Canada's Best Managed Companies is the country's leading business awards program, recognizing excellence in Canadian-owned and -managed companies with revenues over $10 million. Every year, hundreds of entrepreneurial companies compete for this designation in a rigorous and independent process that evaluates the calibre of their management abilities and practice. The program has been recognizing top-performing enterprises through an evaluation process that extends well beyond raw financial results. It is unique among corporate recognition programs in emphasizing a broad range of management capabilities, and in recognizing a company as a whole, and not just senior executives. Currently, it is sponsored by Deloitte, the Canadian Imperial Bank of Commerce (CIBC), the *National Post*, and Queen's School of Business.

Companies can apply for consideration themselves or be nominated by others. In either case, the companies that do make the annual list of Canada's 50 Best Managed Companies must proceed through a rigorous two-phase application process and a business review, and be selected by an independent panel of judges.

Here are the current standards for consideration in the Phase I portion of the program:

- Companies must have annual revenues greater than $10 million.
- They must have superior results for the past three years (e.g., profitability, growth, adapting to changing market conditions).
- They must be Canadian-owned, closely held (generally less than one hundred shareholders) private companies, including portfolio companies controlled by Canadian venture capital and private equity (PE) firms, or Canadian-owned public companies or income trusts with no more than 50 percent of their shares or units traded. A portfolio company must be Canadian based and controlled by Canadian principals. Where a portfolio company is controlled by a pension fund whose investment is managed by a Canadian PE firm, the pension fund must be registered in Canada.

Successful Phase I applicants are notified and invited to proceed to Phase II. Companies are then asked to present in their own words how they develop strategy, demonstrate corporate strengths, excel in their marketplace, retain top talent, and manage business risks. During Phase II, Deloitte and CIBC professionals or "coaches" work with the company every step of the way, providing professional advice and counsel on their presentation.

The detailed assessment and interviews with the awards program coaches for Phase II are then submitted to the final adjudication panel. For the most recent awards, this panel consisted of the following:

- **GARRY FOSTER** is the vice-chair of Deloitte in Canada. With over thirty years of experience in public accounting (twenty-five of those years as a partner), he is considered a leader in the area of board governance, and he completed the Institute of Corporate Directors program in March 2008. His experience includes advising companies on governance, mergers, acquisitions, and financing activities, as well as providing accounting, tax, and business advisory services. From 1998 to 2006, Garry led Deloitte's Canadian Technology, Media and Telecommunications (TMT) practice. He is a member of the Deloitte Canada board of directors, chairs the compensation committee, and is the past chair of the governance and succession planning committees. He is also represents the Canadian firm on the Deloitte US board of directors. Garry is very active in community affairs and is chair of the board of governors of the Friends of Simon Wiesenthal and a member of the board of trustees of the Baycrest Foundation.

- **JON HOUNTALAS** is executive vice-president, Business Banking, at CIBC. He joined CIBC in 2010 and is responsible for all areas of business lending and deposits, including strategy, sales, product development, and the customer experience. Prior to joining CIBC, he spent twenty-five years at HSBC Bank Canada in various client-facing, head office, and executive roles. He holds bachelor of commerce and MBA degrees from McGill University. He is a board member at the York University Foundation and a trustee of the Jewish General Hospital Foundation.
- **THERESA TEDESCO** has worked at the *Globe and Mail*, *Maclean's* magazine, and the *Financial Times*, and has written numerous magazine articles for various Canadian publications. She was a business specialist for the CBC business program *Venture* and is currently a regular commentator on CBC radio. Tedesco was a member of the weekly business panel on CBC

radio's *Morningside* with Peter Gzowski and a guest panelist on TVOntario's *Studio Two*. She has also authored the best-selling book *Offside: The Battle for Control of Maple Leaf Gardens*. As chief business correspondent at the *National Post*, Tedesco spends most of her time working on investigative pieces, which have received journalistic acclaim and award nominations.

- **LUC VILLENEUVE**, FCA, is chair of Samson Bélair/Deloitte & Touche, vice-chair of Deloitte & Touche LLP, co-chair of the national Brand Task Force, member of the Client Council, and member of the Deloitte Foundation. In addition to his managerial role, Luc sits on many boards of different organizations in the province of Quebec. These positions include chair of the board for the Institute of Corporate Directors—Quebec Chapter, member of the board of ICD National, and treasurer of the Quebec Chamber of Commerce Federation. He is also very active with fundraising activities for large not-for-profit organizations.

- **KEN WONG** is one of Canada's most respected marketing professors. He has worked with the Strategic Planning Institute at Harvard University and the Conference Board of Canada, writes a regular column for *Strategy*, *Canadian Grocer*, and *Meetings & Incentive Travel* magazines, and contributes to *Marketing* magazine. He is a 2006 inductee into the Canadian Marketing Hall of Legends and a past winner of the *National Post*'s Leaders in Management Education award. He regularly judges Canada's Best Managed Companies and other competitions, addresses corporations and conventions around the world, and sits on a number of advisory/directorship boards. He is also vice-president, knowledge development, with Level 5 Brand Consulting Inc.

Each year the program's judges select fifty new winners, which are unranked. Previous winners can continue to be recognized in the program through the following designations:

- **Requalified** member: Repeat winners retain their Best Managed Companies designation for an additional two years, subject to an annual operational and financial review.
- **Gold Standard** member: After three consecutive years of maintaining their Best Managed status, companies must reapply to another rigorous two-phase process to achieve Gold Standard member status, subject to an annual operational and financial review.
- **Platinum Club** member: Companies that maintain Best Managed Companies status for six consecutive years are invited to apply to the Platinum Club. This achievement is the pinnacle of the program's recognition.

# 1

# STRATEGY: BREWING UP A WINNING FORMULA FOR MARKETPLACE SUCCESS

When Michael Micovcin arrived in Saskatoon in late 2008 as the new executive vice-president and COO of Great Western Brewing, he leapt out of the frying pan of brand competition in Canada and straight into the fire. Micovcin had enjoyed a long career in large, consumer-product multinationals, including PepsiCo Canada. "The soft drink business is a competitive, tough, mature industry," he says. "Beer is that, and more."

Micovcin (who would become CEO in January 2011) had been fighting in Canada's consumer brand wars since the early 1980s. In 1986, he left Kraft/General Foods to join PepsiCo Canada, and spent fifteen years there, dealing with brands and consumer leadership as well as bottling operations. After several years with Maple Leaf Foods and an entrepreneurial marketing services company, he arrived at Great Western Brewing as the beer industry in Canada was entering a fresh phase of heightened competition. In 2005, Montreal's venerable Molson Breweries had merged with American industry giant Coors, while Labatt Breweries' Belgian-based parent, Interbrew, merged with Brazilian-based AmBev, which subsequently acquired U.S. giant Anheuser-Busch, the brewer of Budweiser. In 2006, Sapporo Breweries Ltd. of Japan acquired Canada's Sleeman Breweries Ltd.

The struggle for market share was about to place downward pricing pressure on mainstream brands. About 80 percent of the Canadian beer market was held by Molson-Coors and Labatt's. The other 20 percent was tremendously fragmented and intensely competitive. That, and more, was unfolding as Micovcin arrived in Saskatoon to take charge of a regional brewery with a limited brand portfolio, a heavy reliance on contract manufacturing, and some concerns over quality control in the minds of customers. The company needed a strategic plan to turn itself around and meet its goal of becoming "the most respected and recognized regional brewery in Canada." It was time for Great Western to live up to the promise of its name.

● ● ●

Strategic planning is something companies often think they engage in, but don't actually do. There's much more to creating a strategic plan than crafting a mission statement, or setting quarterly sales targets or marketing budgets. Managing a company day-to-day can be an extremely complex process, but a winning strategic plan tends to be elegantly simple in identifying specific objectives based on market conditions; in executing the plan, the company defines the metrics that will measure success, the steps to be taken, the time frame for execution, and any necessary changes with an organization. The simpler the stated strategic objectives, in language and number, the more likely a company will not only achieve them, but also understand them as an organization. This places considerable responsibility on leadership to get an organization from top to bottom to focus on strategic objectives—to be on the same page where the company's direction and success criteria are concerned. Strategic leaders among Canada's Best Managed Companies have shown that they know how to design a game plan, and most important, how to engage an organization as a team in order to execute that plan. They know how to play, and they know how to win.

A strategic planning process implies by its definition that a company wishes to "change the game" in a competitive landscape. A significant motivator for established companies is uncertainty, which can truly bring out the "strategic" in the plan. Increased global competitiveness and the challenges of managing an economic downturn can require strategic plans that are defensive in nature. Technological development has meant that barriers to entry in some industries have been lowered, and where this creates opportunities for new players, it demands a nimble response from established ones. Whether plans are defensive or offensive, we've seen a greater demand for agility in their formulation and execution in order to maintain a competitive advantage or to exploit a narrow window of opportunity.

In this chapter, we meet five companies whose industries range from veterinary and health care to brewing and financial services, and who are regional to national players in their respective industries. We show them executing strategic plans at different stages of a company's history. Three are companies that were launched with a winning plan. Another is a company that had enjoyed early successes and was recognized for its management excellence, but required a new strategic plan to realign its offerings with customer expectations. Another is a company with a long history and an urgent need to reinvigorate itself: Great Western Brewing.

Under a new leader, Great Western was able to identify its own shortcomings as well as opportunities in an intensively competitive and mature industry. The market nevertheless was not static, and Great Western had to identify an opportunity in a changing consumer brandscape and use it to drive change throughout the organization.

Michael Micovcin reflects on some of the differences between the mass-market beverages of soft drinks and beer. "The beer industry is a lot more volatile than soft drinks." It is also highly regulated—for one thing, there is no minimum legal drinking age for PepsiCo's Mug root beer or Aquafina bottled water—and those regulations vary from province to province. The retailing environments also differ. Most provinces, for example, have some kind of lowest-price regulation. A zero-tolerance attitude to drinking and driving is also changing the way the product is consumed and sold.

The profile of the typical beer drinker is also changing. "The beer industry is focused on a male demographic of early to late twenties," he notes. But beer consumption is declining. "The industry is shrinking, and the fight for market share is more intense than ever. Beer drinkers are getting older. It is no longer a sexy beverage for younger drinkers, and the industry is looking for ways to innovate the beer category."

To chart a course forward through an increasingly difficult industry, Micovcin began a strategic planning process on his arrival. He knew Great Western Brewing could never go head-to-head with Canada's major brewers—Labatt and Molson-Coors. Great Western needed to identify its competitive differences, and so define where it needed to focus. The company decided it could be successful in two areas, both tied to its regional nature. It could be much more customer-centric than competitors trying to sell brands nationally. And it could brew with recipes that are specific to Western Canada, which prefers smoother beers.

The strategic plan delineated six imperatives (or "pillars") that would guide the company's focus and resources for the coming years. The company would optimize its brand portfolio, build and execute a program to optimize the quality of all Great Western products, build a high-performance sales team, build operational excellence and resources for growth, build and develop organization capabilities, and build information and system capabilities. All six imperatives were critical, but the growth and success of the company depended on revamping the brand portfolio and delivering consistent quality across it.

The beer market is divided into three broad sectors. There are the value/discount brands, which brewers sometimes produce under contract. While they're popular with price-conscious consumers, margins are thin. Next are the mainstream brands—the Coors Lights, the Labatt Blues—with national retailing and heavy marketing support. The third category is reserved for premium or "craft" brews. These are beers that have a more refined brewing process and distinctive taste profiles aimed at niche consumers rather than the broad masses.

In the course of developing the strategic plan, management recognized weaknesses in Great Western's brand portfolio. "The first thing we focused on was the volume/product mix. We had a portfolio skewed to the low end of the market, including a heavy reliance on contract manufacturing. More than half of our business was in that discount market. We had nothing in the 'special occasion' category."

The "special occasion" category included the pricier craft brews as well as higher-end imports. The strategic planning's analysis underscored the fact that beer drinkers are not monolithic in their tastes. They have what Micovcin calls "a dance card of three to five brands." Just as wine drinkers might consume a basic table wine with everyday meals but serve a premium varietal when guests arrive, beer drinkers can also kick up their tastes a notch when company calls. But Great Western didn't have that special-occasion choice in its product mix. "We needed a portfolio that allowed us to compete in all segments across the market," says Micovcin.

The company resolved to do more than plug a gap in the product mix. In creating a special-occasion beer, it could drive many of the goals of the strategic plan. Such a beer would be a flagship brand that enhanced the company's name and reputation across the brand portfolio and the geographic market it was serving. The special-occasion beer would be a premium brew that would target consumers over the age of thirty. "These are slightly more sophisticated and discretionary drinkers," says Micovcin. They weren't the late-twenties males that the mainstream and discount brands were chasing. That was a market Great Western still needed to address with other brands in its portfolio, but competition was increasingly ferocious. As Great Western embarked on its strategic planning, the big brewers especially were becoming anxious about the rise of discount brands and their razor-thin margins, and were moving to reduce the price difference between discounts and their mainstream brands. In Alberta, Micovcin watched as the price difference between twenty-four discount beers and the same number of Coors Light fell from about ten dollars to two to three dollars. The new flagship brand would satisfy a host of strategic goals. It would meet the corporate objective of being a strong regional player by providing a premium beer crafted for western tastes. It would continue the drive for quality improvement throughout the product line. The company had suffered from inconsistent production in the mid-1990s, and as Micovcin says, "The consumer has a long memory." The quality that Great Western has delivered by focusing on achieving consistency throughout the product line was a necessity for corporate survival, not an option. "As a local brewery, our beer should be the freshest and most consistent."

A new flagship brand would also assert the brand name of Great Western Brewing, which was not well known outside its home province. "We were Saskatoon-centric. Brand awareness outside the city began to slide." In Alberta, the brewery was known for its discount Brewhouse brand. "We had poor recognition as Great Western."

The new flagship brand could also elevate the profile of Great Western Brewing by being *about* Great Western Brewing. Beer is one of those consumer products that benefits (as we see later in this chapter, when we meet Steam Whistle Brewery of Toronto) from an underlying narrative, a story that assures the consumer the product is part of a craft manufacturing tradition. It is especially important with a regional brewer. The product needs to convey local character and local roots. And Great Western, says Micovcin, "has a great story." It needed a premium beer that could tell it.

The brewery was founded in 1927 as Hub City Brewing Co. It changed its name to Western Canada Brewing Company in 1930, and then became Drewery's Ltd. in 1932. It was bought by O'Keefe in 1956, and carried on as part of Carling O'Keefe until 1989, when Carling O'Keefe was acquired by Molson. In the process, Molson announced the Saskatoon brewery was slated for closure as the new owner rationalized production capacity.

To save the brewery and its jobs, sixteen front-line employees, aided by a note from the government of Saskatchewan, stepped forward to acquire the brewery and start operating it as Great Western Brewing. In the late 1990s, the government note was retired through a fresh round of investment, and the company carried on with a fairly stable ownership structure.

The rescue of the brewery spoke volumes about community pride. The new beer would remind consumers of that increasingly distant event and amplify it by showcasing a local pride in craft. "We wanted to be known as 'A brewer with heart.' We have to connect with our consumers by playing our local card, if you will."

The new product would be a premium double-aged pale ale created for discerning Western Canadian palates. It was called "Original 16." The tribute to the employees who rescued the brewery in 1989 played nicely on the Original Six teams of the NHL in a market with strong hockey enthusiasm.

It may have seemed a precarious time for Great Western to make a move into this segment. While the discounting in mainstream brands has closed their gap with discount brands, at the same time it has opened a further price gap between mainstream and premium. But the special-occasion consumer is older and less price sensitive and has been willing to pay a premium price for a premium product that is a "special occasion" treat. Micovcin says Great Western has further product plans in that end.

Great Western's strategy exemplified the nimbleness companies today need to exploit opportunities amid a host of competitive uncertainties and fluid business conditions. Launched in March 2011, Original 16 was an immediate and "phenomenal" success, says Micovcin. "Original 16 was less for Saskatchewan than it was for building the company outside of our province. The goal was to introduce a reputational brand that would also introduce Great Western Brewing to all of Western Canada. Beyond profits, it's given us credibility to do things we couldn't have done five or ten years ago. It effectively launched Great Western Brewing for the first time in Alberta. It has exceeded all our expectations."

● ● ●

Where Great Western had to develop and rapidly execute a new strategic plan to reverse the fortunes of an established company in a volatile, competitive climate, Concentra Financial is a young enterprise that only a few years after its creation needed to move with similar speed and decisiveness to correct its course and recalibrate its relationship with its customers.

Although Concentra was officially founded in 2005, it has deep roots in its industry. One founding element was Co-operative Trust, a financial institution specializing in business-to-business financial and trust services that supplied credit unions nationwide with financial intermediary and trusteeship services, including registered plans. The other element was the commercial business lines of Credit Union Central of Saskatchewan (SaskCentral), a trade association for Saskatchewan credit unions that manages statutory liquidity and provides trade association services; it is also Concentra's major shareholder.

Responding to a new federal initiative to allow credit unions to operate nationally under the Cooperative Credit Associations Act, the founding organizations of Concentra Financial saw an opportunity to restructure themselves in a new venture that would extend the Saskatchewan-based services across the country and promote nationwide growth in the Canadian credit union system. Concentra provides solutions to credit unions in two key areas. One is corporate financial solutions and financial management consulting, which supports day-to-day credit union operations, excess liquidity management and investments, and risk management. The other is trust solutions, offered by wholly owned subsidiary Concentra Trust, ranging from estate planning and administration to the delivery of registered plans and specialized corporate trusts.

During the first few years of its existence, Concentra merged two corporate cultures to create a single company. It then had to weather the 2007–08 recession. Its management excellence earned it a place in the Platinum Club of Canada's Best Managed Companies in 2009. As Concentra exited the recession, it had fundamental issues to address that required a new strategic focus over a relatively short, three-year period.

"We had to ask ourselves three things," says Ken Kosolofski, Concentra's CEO. "Do we have market relevance in the credit union system? Do we have a sustainable return on investment? And do we have sound business practices?" Pursuing positive answers to those questions became Concentra's three core strategies. As Kosolofski summarizes, Concentra decided to focus on bringing value to credit unions rather than extracting it from the system. Its relationships with more than three hundred Canadian credit unions through trustee business demonstrate such value, as do the leasing operations. Yet where market relevance in the credit union system was concerned, Concentra needed to address actual as well as perceived competition between its own marketplace activities and the credit unions that it was designed to support.

In its corporate banking activities, Concentra would deal directly with commercial businesses, at the same time that credit unions were doing commercial deals. There was also market conflict between Concentra and credit unions in the mortgage broker market.

"Credit unions were pushing back," says Kosolofski. "We wanted to refocus, to retain market-relevance for our credit union partners." As Kosolofski also notes: "Out in the retail marketplace we are just part of the general market noise—but in the credit union market space we are a single voice."

True to its strategy, Concentra decided that it would not be active on the retail side unless the credit unions themselves requested it, but would focus solely on providing solutions to and through credit unions. It exited the mortgage broker market and restructured its commercial lending, helping credit unions with their business and transferring relationships back to them. It also changed its approach to the deposit market. It continues to require deposit funds to provide services to credit union clients, but has amended its retail deposit business model to focus on alternative funding sources that are less costly and do not put Concentra in the position of being in competition with its credit union clients.

On the question of whether Concentra can show a sustainable return on investment, Kosolofski says, "We've been able to say yes for three years so far. It's a good start for sustainable profitability, above 10 percent return on equity."

And on the question of improving business practices, Kosolofski states: "We're getting rid of silos and functioning as a cohesive business unit. We're consolidating multiple banking systems, the backbone of our operations. From 2010 to 2012, we worked really hard on our strategy execution process. It's made us much more intentional in style for executing strategy."

Looking ahead, "We have to be sure everything we do brings value to the credit union system, and we have to continue to evolve our approaches as the needs of credit unions continue to change," says Kosolofski. "The feedback we've heard so far is positive and we to need to continue that trend. We'll keep asking: 'Where do we see ourselves five years out?'"

● ● ●

Look closely at the base of a bottle of Steam Whistle Pilsner and you can just make out, moulded into the glass, the figures 3FG. They are the manufacturing equivalent of what computer game enthusiasts call an "Easter egg"—a hidden clue to the story of Steam Whistle

Brewing. In the business plan drawn up by Cameron (Cam) Heaps, Greg Cromwell, and Greg Taylor in 1999, they proposed calling their new venture the Three Fired Guys Brewing Company. It was about the only aspect of their business proposal that didn't become reality. But the fact that Steam Whistle was indeed founded by three guys let go by Sleeman Breweries after it bought their employer, Upper Canada Brewing Company, in 1998, is part of the abundantly storied history of a young venture in an old craft tradition.

"People like hearing stories," says co-founder Greg Taylor, who oversees day-to-day operations, "so a company has got to have a good story. And the story of the 'three fired guys' rings true, and people like it."

Steam Whistle is a fascinating case of a company whose story and strategic plan are locked in a feedback loop: The story is the basis of its strategic plan, and the unfolding of the strategic plan continues to fuel the story. And because Steam Whistle is in the business of producing beer, one of the most brand-conscious consumer products, the strategic plan is entwined in the process of defining the entire company according to the virtues of its brand.

Steam Whistle would not be a success without its well-received premium Pilsner lager, double-decoction brewed to a Czech recipe by its Czech-born brewmaster, which has been named Best Pilsner at the Ontario Brewing Awards four times. It is the only beer Steam Whistle has ever brewed and ever plans to brew. The company also follows a rigorous planning and reportage rubric that includes taste tests, consumer feedback, daily media monitoring, and weekly reviews of sales by channel, package size, and container type. But it's the story of Steam Whistle that is at the heart of the company's strategic plan, which is based on three pillars.

One pillar is the foundation story—how three guys in the beer business who no longer had jobs went back into the beer business.

Another is the beer—what Steam Whistle makes and why it makes this beer and nothing else. And the third is the brewery itself—the remarkable building near Toronto's CN Tower that was once a locomotive roundhouse. The building was the missing ingredient when the business plan was created. Without that particular building, Steam Whistle might not even be here today. It is, as Greg Taylor says, "our Cathedral of Beer."

Steam Whistle has accumulated a veritable trophy case of accolades. To name a few: It earned its fourth successive honour as one of Canada's Best Managed Companies in 2011 and in 2010 was a regional winner of Canada's 10 Most Admired Corporate Cultures, in addition to being named one of Canada's Greenest Employers. Much of the success story of Steam Whistle lies in its back story, in the roots of this start-up in the Upper Canada Brewing Company, which had been launched by Cam Heaps's father, Frank Heaps, in 1984.

Greg Taylor was working as a bike courier in Toronto when his wife Sybil Taylor (who now handles communications for Steam Whistle) invited him to come work with her at Upper Canada in 1988. Over the next ten years, Greg Taylor rose to vice-president of sales, while Sybil became vice-president of development and distribution, but the last few years had seen a steady dilution of Upper Canada's cachet in a series of ownership changes. Steam Whistle in many ways is a reboot of Upper Canada, with its principals and investors well aware of the formula that worked so well in the original company and what the consequences had been of that plan going awry.

Upper Canada was a pioneering craft brewer in Ontario, whose success in introducing premium domestic beer, made in small batches, changed the Canadian brewing industry. It was at the forefront of a host of start-ups, including Sleeman Breweries of

Guelph, Ontario, which was established in 1988. But in the 1990s, Upper Canada had begun to lose its way. New investors came along: Corby Distillers took a 40 percent interest in 1991 and then sold its share to Hurlow Partners and Penfund Investment Corp. in 1995. In 1996, Upper Canada went public with a $25 million IPO, but after the stock began trading at $8 in March and reached a high of $8.50, it fell to $4 by year-end, and Frank Heaps departed as CEO, as did Sybil Taylor. In 1998, Sleeman acquired Upper Canada for $27 million and the three guys were out of work as the Upper Canada operation in Toronto was closed down and production moved to Sleeman's plant in Guelph. (Sleeman still brews two Upper Canada brands, but Sleeman in turn was acquired by Sapporo Brewery of Japan in 2006. Upper Canada Lager and Dark Ale are now discount brands.)

The denouement of Upper Canada Brewery as an independent craft brewer provided an abundance of lessons reflected in Steam Whistle's determinedly simple strategy. In 1992, for example, Upper Canada abandoned its distinctive bottles without screw caps to adopt the new tall-boy bottle with screw cap introduced as the industry standard in 1991. Steam Whistle's signature bottles in contrast are highly distinctive—green glass with a painted (not paper) label, in a shape that pays tribute to the industry-standard beer and soda-pop bottle of the 1950s, and you need a bottle opener to get at the contents. Steam Whistle's decision to brew just one type of beer is informed by a runaway launching of new brands that had occurred at Upper Canada. As Sybil Taylor recalls, Upper Canada had as many as twenty-one different brands at one point, but 55 percent of sales were being generated by its signature Lager and another 30 percent by its Dark Ale. That left nineteen other brands producing 15 percent of sales, which was an excessive burden on marketing, sales, and production.

One of Upper Canada's great assets had been its brewery, established in an old warehouse on Atlantic Avenue in Toronto's west end. Customers loved touring it, and the presence of a gift shop meant it was allowed to sell beer on the premises. When Sleeman moved production to Guelph, the Upper Canada brands lost an element of their attraction to craft brewing enthusiasts. The founders of Steam Whistle, who had all worked in the old Upper Canada facility, understood that the brewery itself was critical to the strategic plan. While they abandoned the idea of the Three Fired Guys name, they still wanted to invoke a working man's craft ethic and came up with the name Steam Whistle, inspired by the factory whistles of a bygone era signalling the end of an honest day's work. But they couldn't find the brewery site they knew they needed.

"Generally, people don't like to tour yogurt plants," says Greg Taylor. "And they're not interested in seeing where brakes are made. But when it comes to brewing beer, they have a real passion for that. If you can combine that brewery experience with story-telling, it allows people to make a connection."

The most resonant advice came from Greg Mahon, who had brought premium home-made ice cream to Toronto when he founded Greg's Ice Cream in 1981. The three fired guys had gotten to know him because of a beer-flavoured ice cream that Mahon concocted during their Upper Canada days. "We were struggling to find a building," Greg Taylor recalls. "And Greg said, 'Remember, you have to find your Cathedral of Beer. It must inspire people when they come in.' And he was right."

They had all but given up hope of finding the right building when they happened upon the John Street Roundhouse, built in 1929, which once serviced the locomotives of the Canadian Pacific Railway. A listed Toronto historic property, eleven of its bays had been dismantled during the construction of the south (below-ground) extension of the Metro Toronto Convention Centre and then reassembled. It was sitting empty, waiting for someone to come forward with a plan for it that satisfied both the city of Toronto and TrizecHahn, which operated the adjacent CN Tower and was responsible for finding tenants for the Roundhouse.

"We already had chosen the name 'Steam Whistle' a few months earlier," Sybil Taylor explains. "We'd even had the logo designed for our business plan. So when they came upon the Roundhouse, which was a locomotive repair ship … all the forces were just bringing us together."

A key figure in getting Steam Whistle started was Frank Heaps, whom the three fired guys wanted on board. "He'd had some bad experiences with the end of Upper Canada," says Greg Taylor. "He wasn't happy about getting back in the beer business. But we called him into the meeting at TrizecHahn about the Roundhouse." Afterwards, Greg Taylor had lunch with Cam and his father Frank. "Cam's dad said, 'We've got to get that building.' Then I knew: Frank's in."

"With Frank," Sybil Taylor notes, "came a lot of investors, and a lot of confidence in us from the city. The 3FG were good, and we'd all worked in the beer industry for about decade. But Cam was twenty-four, and Greg and I were both thirty-four. Having Frank and that building were key components." Today Frank Heaps is chair of the board, while Cam Heaps and Greg Taylor are officially "co-founders" with an equal minority interest. (The third fired guy, Greg Cromwell, helped to write the business plan but shortly thereafter moved to Australia. He served for a time as a director, but he did not work in its operations, and he retains a small holding in the company.)

With the Roundhouse came the business's centre of gravity, a historic building in the heart of a burgeoning downtown area with attractions like the CN Tower, Harbourfront, the theatre district, the Convention Centre, and the Rogers Centre all close at hand. The Roundhouse is also part of the Toronto Railway Heritage Centre. It is a note-perfect setting for an enterprise dedicated to an industrial craft, and tours are so popular that the company has installed second-story catwalks in the brewhouse and bottle shop to keep the steady stream of visitors clear of the production bustle.

In 2002, a freelancing consultant interviewed 200 people on the street and proposed to Steam Whistle to tell the company what he had learned. They gave him a hearing (and paid him for his time).

"We were told people knew two things about us," Greg Taylor says. "We had a brewery in the Roundhouse, and we only made one beer." Rather than view those facts as warning signs of competitive limitations, Steam Whistle has embraced them strategically as their defining characteristics. The company's slogan is "Do one thing, really, really well." That thing is to "make one beer of exceptional quality that Canadians can be proud of" and to make it in the Roundhouse. The beer, the building, and the commitment to craft excellence are inextricably entwined in Steam Whistle's strategic plan.

Its beer is now sold in Ontario, Alberta, and British Columbia. Steam Whistle's goal is to become known as the brewer of Canada's most respected premium beer. When it gets there, it will make for a great story.

• • •

Strategic plans are demanded when companies find themselves in dire competitive straits. Moments of crisis also inspire strategic plans, creating new companies as opportunities emerge in response. In the late 1970s, the veterinary industry was facing such a crisis.

The "companion animals" sector of the business, mainly focused on dogs and cats, had been following the same model since the 1950s. Communities were home to small practices staffed by one or two vets. Generally one vet would own the practice and he or she would take on a younger associate. The standard succession plan was that the older vet would sell the practice to the associate and then retire. But vets were increasingly finding that this tried-and-true model was no longer working.

"Some industries get locked in time, and then forces of change suddenly overtake them," says David Farran.

Farran had no idea there was a growing problem in the Canadian veterinary business until he was invited to lunch with two vets who were part of a three-vet partnership, Associate Veterinary Clinics, which owned a major veterinary hospital in Calgary. The third vet was retiring, which raised the general issue of how the old model of succession in veterinary care was breaking down.

Farran is not a vet himself. He has an MBA, is a past vice-president of Calgary's Big Rock Brewery, once owned a small travel agency chain, and foremost served as vice-consul for Britain in Western Canada. But he is also a confirmed pet owner. He currently has two dogs (a black lab and a dachshund), a cat, and seven horses. "As I heard about the changes in the industry," he recalls, "I was inspired." Farran got involved in the succession situation at Associate Veterinary Clinics, taking on the position of the third vet when he retired and the role of CEO in 2003. Farran set himself to building a strategic plan for the company that was also a new strategic plan for a significant number of Canadian veterinary clinics, as the renaissance of Associate Veterinary Clinics turned to expansion.

For many clinics, the old succession model had broken down along two fault lines. The first was that the old vet clinic was becoming an endangered species. Clinics increasingly were becoming small hospitals, in response to greater levels of care that companion pet owners were demanding. "Pets are more important in people's lives," says Farran. As families in general have fewer children, and as the therapeutic value of pets has become recognized, these dogs and cats "have acquired elevated status in the household. That has created a huge demand for elevated services. People say, 'I want for my pet what I can get for myself.' And the services to meet that demand weren't there."

With that increased service demand, the typical veterinary clinic became far more expensive to equip, maintain, and staff than it had ever been. The skyrocketing capital intensity of clinics thus helped trigger the succession crisis. Buying out a retiring owner was far more expensive than before. In addition to an array of expensive medical equipment, clinics were becoming physically larger and far more expensive as real estate. New vets looking to buy out an old-style vet practice were also confronting considerable investments to bring a practice up to the higher standards pet owners were demanding.

At the same time, veterinary schools were experiencing a dramatic demographic change. Ninety-five percent of graduates destined for companion-pet care were women, and not enough of them were willing or able to take on the debt burdens the old succession model demanded.

Someone else looking in from the outside—a banking executive, perhaps—might propose that the solution lay in finding more creative ways to finance the new owner of the practice. Farran, however, could see that a fundamental disinterest in being burdened by acquisition debt meant that it wouldn't be enough to patch over problems in the standard clinic ownership model. Clinics needed an entirely different business model. His new venture's strategic plan would be theirs as well. "We saw the future of the community practice," he says. "That practice wasn't going to go away, but it was going to change dramatically."

Farran addressed the succession problem with a solution that was sensitive to the traditions of the industry, the needs of its retiring vets and newly trained ones, and the expectations of its customers. Associate owns or co-owns more than forty-five clinics and hospitals, but none of them carry the company name. They are all individually branded, like a traditional clinic. There is no need for an overarching brand identifying all Associate clinics by a single name for consumers, and there are good reasons to avoid doing so. The main reason is that pet owners remain attached to the idea of the local clinic, and many would be reluctant to take their dog or cat to any clinic that seemed to be a chain operation. "The clinics retain their names and signage, because customers are still looking for their community vet," says Farran. "A single entity, we feel, would cheapen the brand."

Associate has pursued a two-pronged strategy. It provides an exit for a retiring vet, and a compelling business operating model for associate vets who are already working in the clinic or are graduating from veterinary college and seeking a practice opportunity that doesn't hew to the old acquisition model. It would make no sense for Associate to acquire veterinary clinics if it wasn't able to make a case for vets to staff them. In fact, given the hostility with which Associate's plan was initially greeted by many members of the veterinary profession, acquiring clinics would have been impossible if it could not make an effective case for its new business model.

The basic acquisition model is for Associate to acquire a practice, but not the bricks-and-mortar real estate. "Often the retiring vet will continue to own the building," says Farran. That makes the acquisition less expensive for Associate and also allows the retiring vet to continue to enjoy an income stream from the ongoing clinic's rental of the property. The acquired clinics retain their name and signage. Nothing outwardly changes about them at all, where the consumer is concerned. For that matter, the pet owner is unlikely to encounter a significant change in the staff: Farran says Associate has a 97 percent retention rate on vets who were already working at acquired clinics.

"The industry viewed us with great suspicion. We heard: 'Who are you to come in and say how to run a clinic?' We had to prove up you could separate management from medicine." That was the crux of Associate's proposition to the vets who would work as Associate employees, in clinics that Associate now owned. Associate would bring efficiencies to the business. It would not tell vets how to practise medicine or interact with pet owners. If anything, it could improve veterinary care by removing burdens of management and permitting staff to focus on medicine, and by providing state-of-the-art equipment and ongoing training.

"One of the keys to our strategy is we do invest in people," says Farran. Associate has also invested in new technology, such as one that allows clinics to share real-time x-rays, MRIs and CT scans over the Web and tap the expertise of specialists. A radiologist in Calgary can consult with a vet in Toronto, advising on how to position a dog as an image is being collected digitally. Associate's own neurologists can ask a veterinarian to examine a patient by webcam so the vet can see neurologic symptoms over the Web. Associate can thus leverage its collective expertise, regardless of location, using a technology that had never been incorporated into veterinary practice.

Associate has secured efficiencies in part by deploying a hub-and-spoke model of acquisition and expansion. It has focused growth on several hubs: Ottawa, London, Calgary, Vancouver, and Victoria. In 2011, Associate acquired Ottawa's Alta Vista, the second-largest veterinary hospital in Canada, which greatly enhanced its reputation in the profession. The hub-and-spoke model increases Associate's local market share, and it allows clinics to share resources, such as maintenance staff and "locum" or fill-in vets. "Orphan" clinics would be neglected.

Farran says a key strategic component in executing the business plan was that "we pre-invested in the management team. When we went to buy clinics, we were prepared to run them, and not to play catch-up. It was a hard convincing act, to persuade investors that we had to hire the management team first before we had the revenues from clinics. We said, 'We can't falter. We need an effective management team in advance.'" Investors agreed, and Farran proudly recalls, "We hit every target we ever aimed at. As we added clinics, the economies of scale kicked in and we essentially grew into our oversize suit. We're a $105 million company now. At 4 percent, we have the lowest ratio of overhead to revenues of any North American veterinary company, and we don't anticipate having to change that."

● ● ●

In veterinary care, David Farran found a strategic business opportunity based on an industry model of succession that was breaking down. Where the well-being of pets' owners is concerned, CBI Health Group evolved from one specialized patient-care facility to create a nationwide network of health-care services. CBI Health Group was already inside the health-care system when it recognized fresh opportunities for growth. Its success resides in a strategic plan that is highly disciplined in defining and pursuing those growth opportunities.

The company's goal "is to be respected as a leader in building integrated health teams in community care," says CEO Christopher Szybbo. "It's not solely to be the largest in scale. And we focus on integration, not diversification. All of our services have got to be working together cohesively."

In a country that prides itself in public health care, the degree to which the Canadian system is actually private may come as a surprise. "The general public often thinks Canada has a largely publicly funded health-care system," Szybbo observes. "In fact, about 30 percent of the system is privately funded." The areas of "self-pay" and "third-party pay" (for example, extended health insurance) are experiencing growth and proliferation. It's in this significant aspect of Canadian health-care services that CBI has established a respected and expanding presence.

The company began as the Canadian Back Institute, opening its first facility in 1984 dedicated to neck and back problems. As the services it offered became more generalized, the name was changed to CBI Health in 1997. In 2009, the company became CBI Health Group—the word "Group" was added to show "this is a growing network of health-care services and facilities across Canada," says Szybbo.

Today, CBI Health Group provides care in the areas of physio, occupational, exercise, speech and behavioural therapies, as well as physician, chiropractic, nursing, massage, home health, and elder-care. Those services are organized into a network that includes more than 145 interdisciplinary clinics in eight provinces. It also operates walk-in medical clinics in British Columbia (called Carepoint Medical Centres) and has units dedicated to home care, eldercare, and pediatric care for autism spectrum disorders. CBI's Assessment Services consists of experts specializing in providing independent health-care assessments. It also has a Workplace Solutions segment, which provides expert health and safety services to reduce risk and injury within the workplace.

CBI has marshalled its expansion through a rigorous set of objectives and principles. The focus on community care is important. "We're not interested in running hospitals and institutions," says Szybbo. "We support the development of public health care. We want to work collectively with it to improve care access and outcomes." To that end, it works with some public hospitals to provide certain patient-care services.

A core strategic objective is to develop a corporate culture capable of responding to strategic opportunities and meeting goals. "The 'organization and culture as strategy' has been written about for some time and this certainly resonates with us," Szybbo notes. "Many strategies seem to focus on the 'what.' But we work to first understand and articulate our purpose as a company—the 'why'—and to build the notion of an internal culture that's execution-driven and focused on high-performance—the 'how.' That way, when we identify the 'what,' we're going to be able to execute. The organization grows the brand because of its execution culture and results-orientation. And critical to this is identifying and developing talent internally."

CBI adheres to a strategic theme map focused on three components. It aims to continually optimize delivery, quality, and operating efficiency; to increase its market share within high-volume customer segments; and to leverage core competencies in order to enter into new customer segments.

That first component—continually optimizing operating efficiency and qualify—is an internal focus, says Szybbo, "but it really starts with the customer. We understand the desired outcomes of customers and work backwards from them to develop the delivery methods." It's a "lean" process like that of manufacturing, and the goal is to build a standard of application that the company can move from site to site across its services network.

"You drive consistency of results with that," says Szybbo. "Health care delivery is very fragmented across Canada. If you're a referral source, why should you choose us? If you've asked how the customer defines value, then that's how you deliver. When you refer someone to CBI, you know exactly what you're going to get. For referrers like insurance companies and workers compensation boards, CBI can be a go-to company, because we've lowered their cost of procurement, with scale, and operating costs, through consistency of quality outcomes."

To drive efficiencies, CBI has developed a highly scalable infrastructure with standardized processes that allow it to establish consistency of application across its service network. "It's a highly measured environment," says Szybbo. A proprietary IT system measures effectiveness, efficiency, productivity, employee engagement, and more.

The second component of the strategic theme map—increasing share within high-volume customer segments—is the basis of CBI's commitment to focusing on community care. "We're not going to be all things to all people." To begin, CBI's service strategy is organized more around business-to-business (B2B) than business-to-consumer (B2C). "Although we have over 1.5 million patient visits a year, we look for places that aggregate patient volume, and make our value proposition to them. We establish a reason for them to choose us," which is the first component of the strategic theme map.

CBI's services growth is always aimed at increasing the value proposition for these patient aggregators. It adds service aligned with procurement. The company is also attuned to fulfillment needs of procurers across large geographies, increasing scale by either acquiring existing facilities and businesses or adding new ("de novo") operations.

The third component of the strategic theme map—leveraging core competencies into new segments—has led it into several new areas of business in recent years. In 2006, CBI introduced home health with eldercare services. Eldercare provides physiotherapy and occupational therapy to elderly patients both at home and in the community, while home health provides a comprehensive range of nursing, therapies, support, and social services to individuals of all ages and abilities within the home environment. In 2009, it established a pediatric-care service called Monarch House in Burnaby, BC, for children with autism spectrum disorders and their families.

"It's exactly what we do in other segments," Szybbo says of Monarch House. "We organize a diverse health-care team into an interdisciplinary approach." In the case of Monarch House, this has been achieved with a pediatrician and psychologist, and services in behavioural therapies, speech and language pathology, and occupational therapy.

CBI's impressive growth has been achieved by a rigorous adherence to its strategic plan. And while the number of facilities has grown 20 percent in the last five years, over the same period average revenues per site have increased 28 percent. "We've more than doubled the size of the company in the last five years," says Szybbo, "and not just by adding dots on a map."

● ● ●

Strategic plans do not always work out as planned. Companies that embark on them need to be alert and nimble enough to recognize when market conditions have changed or premises of a plan are failing to hold up and to adjust their objectives accordingly. But a well-conceived plan requires commitment and support throughout the organization, and it's the responsibility of leadership to convey the need for that commitment and to provide the tools and structure necessary to achieve it.

Leadership is an adjunct to strategy. A company needs to have an *articulated* business strategy, and it must be communicated throughout the organization. For a strategy to be articulated, it must be consistent, clear, and coherent, and it needs leadership capable of articulating it. The strategy's architects must work regularly with the management team to ensure it is being carried out. And a company needs to be grooming the next generation to ensure that there are capable leaders evolving within who are carrying out the current strategy and will be in place to produce and oversee the next one. To that end, leaders must uphold the value of training and development initiatives. Perhaps the most significant advantage of strategic planning is that it can provide goal posts by which both the day-to-day and the life-altering decisions can be made.

For any company embarking on designing and executing a new strategic plan, Concentra Financial's Ken Kosolofski advises: "The key to success is to make sure you're focused. A lot of the financial industry after the recession went back to core businesses. Focus on something you're good at."

If you need to change management or products, then do it, Kosolofski says. He advises developing three core strategies, or mantras, to drive the necessary change. "Simplify what your company needs to focus on. You can't be worried about short-term results as much as the bigger picture of the company itself. And you have to ask yourself how you define success."

# 2

# LEADERSHIP: INVERTING THE PYRAMID TO EMPOWER THE WORKFORCE

When asked to explain Apex Distribution's approach to leadership, Don White, its president, CEO, and co-founder, cites the adage, "If you can't lead, get out of the way." Apex's philosophy in fact might best be put as "If you *can* lead, you're getting out of the way."

Leadership in business is still popularly seen as a purview of individuals, of strong, charismatic personalities leading companies with thousands—even tens of thousands—of employees. It may be particularly the case with public companies, where investors, analysts, and the media seek (and respond positively to) a strong figure at the apex of an organization. Capable, charismatic, and compelling leaders are still highly desired in business (call it the Steve Jobs effect), by private companies as much as public ones, but the concept of leadership is changing. Charisma will only take a leader so far, especially if its sole purpose is to turn employees (and shareholders) into unquestioning followers who look to the top of the management pyramid for inspiration, guidance, and motivation.

The sort of leadership embraced by Apex is proliferating through the ranks of top companies. A number of interrelated factors are contributing to the trend of what we call "collective leadership," and they naturally encompass issues like talent retention and succession planning. Downsizings, whether in response to economic headwinds or increased productivity, have created companies with fewer employees organized in fewer layers. Companies with flatter hierarchies are being led by CEOs with shorter durations at the top. Economic uncertainty, new technology, greater regulatory scrutiny, and global competition are demanding more responsive operations. Management that is simply prescriptive is giving way to organizations that engage their talent pools. The new enterprise is learning to lead itself.

Leadership in Canada's Best Managed Companies more often than not is dedicated to minimizing hierarchy, even to inverting the pyramid so that employees understand they have the power to lead, to act, and to innovate, without waiting for senior management to show the way. In many companies, management becomes concerned with enabling and harnessing that empowerment. Companies and senior executives are learning that it is much easier, and more gratifying and more profitable, to lead a group of collaborators rather than a group of followers—or at worst, a group that forms a wide, heavy base of an immovable pyramid and is even reluctant to follow.

There is no single way to lead a company in the new millennium. Indeed, our research at Deloitte has shown that there are multiple ways of leading. While it's tempting to divide leadership approaches into two categories—"command and control" and "everything else"—we've identified eight leadership models or architectures that organizations can use to foster more effective performance from their talent. Those models are arrayed along two axes. The vertical axis in the following chart ranges from the most directive ("landlord and tenants") to the most emergent ("community organizer and volunteers"). The horizontal axis ranges from the most scripted ("conductor and orchestra") to the most creative ("producer and creative team").

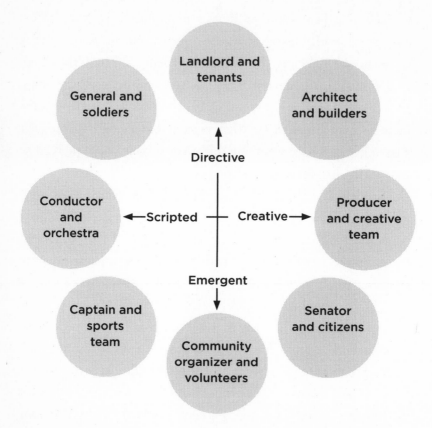

Source: "Human Capital Trends 2011: Revolution/Evolution" by Jeff Schwartz and Marty DiMarzio (Deloitte & Touche).

Each is a model of an organization working as one. Collective leadership reflects a number of these new ways of leading. It builds on a foundation of understanding how employees feel about their organizations—and provides new insights on how to move people into effective action. We believe collective leadership is what happens when a large group of people comes together and commits to making big things happen. With collective leadership, an organization focuses on a single question: What does it take to ensure all of our people are engaged to deliver the business strategy? Collective action is how business leaders are more effectively executing that strategy.

•  •  •

Founded in 1999, Apex Distribution is a young, Calgary-based company with about 475 employees. It distributes industrial and oilfield products and services to business in oil and gas production, mining, forestry, and food processing, as well contractors and service companies associated with these industries. Its products include valves, pumps, pipes, and automation, control, and monitoring systems. Active in all four provinces of Western Canada, in 2010 Apex entered the U.S. market by acquiring Remington Pipe and Supply, now Apex Remington. Two more significant additions were made in 2011. One was a controlling interest in an associated company, Tierra Alta Production Services, which was renamed Apex Advanced Solutions. The other was the acquisition of McAlester Pipe and Supply Ltd. in Oklahoma. After riding out the 2010 downturn in its market (limiting its revenue decrease to 28 percent when the market declined 57 percent), Apex rebounded with a surge in revenue in 2011 that topped its record performance of 2009.

Apex has an empowerment-based leadership style, which has meant communicating and supporting the necessary corporate culture, particularly as the company continues to grow through acquisitions and established enterprises are brought under the Apex umbrella. The mergers and acquisition boom has required organizations to combine quickly. This can require organizations to be stitched together with very different corporate and operational cultures. In Chapter 6, "Mergers and Acquisitions: Making Instead of Breaking, by Matching Cultures," we discuss how companies that have successfully pursued mergers and acquisitions as a growth strategy stress the ultimate importance of matching cultures in acquisition opportunities. But the wave of mergers and acquisitions, which has required some companies to act quickly on opportunities, can result in less than perfect cultural matches. Collective leadership can help mend the seams.

At Apex, all new employees are issued a card that spells out the ten values the company expects them to uphold:

- We are positive and passionate about what we do ☐
- We take our jobs seriously, but not ourselves ☐
- We embrace change and innovation ☐
- We are friendly and caring towards our people and customers ☐
- We treat everyone with respect ☐
- The person doing the job knows best ☐
- Anything can be improved ☐
- The customers' needs are critical ☐
- We work safely ☐
- Quality is everyone's job ☐

It's that sixth point—"The person doing the job knows best"—that underscores Don White's approach to leadership. The key concept is empowerment. "People in the company know their areas better than we do," says White of himself and fellow senior management. "We empower them to do the right thing. We intervene with help and resources."

"We structure the organization to support that strategy,"

adds Greg Abtosway, Apex's COO. "We're employee-owned, and we tend to attract some of the most experienced people in the business." That's important to Apex's approach of letting staff do what they're good at, as Abtosway cautions: "Empowering people without appropriate experience could be dangerous."

Saying employees are "empowered" can be an empty boast if you don't give them the means to act and the resources to do so. "We give them the tools and access to information and risk-taking capabilities to be empowered," Abtosway says. That information includes financial details, both projected and actual, to a degree that might make some companies nervous.

Abtosway says he doesn't worry about giving employees access to financial information because it has such a limited shelf life. Someone could leak data to a competitor and it wouldn't really matter: "It's stale in three months." Apex's leadership is more interested in ensuring that employees have the information necessary for them to excel and carry the company forward with them.

"Compensation is based on results," says Abtosway, "and so everyone is tied to result. Everyone works together to meet a common end. We have a compensation structure that drives opportunity and teamwork."

In 2011, Apex consolidated its different operations and acquisitions under a single information system that provides organization-wide operations, procurement, and accounting visibility, with real-time access to information to support decision-making. "We pay a lot of attention to financial performance. That's our guiding principle," says White.

In the first ten days of every month, the company gathers "best-guess" short-term forecasts of revenues and expenses, along with general comments about what is happening with competitors and customers. That information is then sent out to everyone in the company. Every week, that best-guess forecast is lined up against actual results and shared throughout the organization. "We want people to overachieve, exceeding forecasts by 20 to 30 percent," says White. "By beating the best-guess, you create a winning attitude."

Every two months, the company holds an "Apex Advantage" session. Ten to fifteen employees from all levels gather to hear each member of the executive team discuss their areas of responsibility, direction, and vision. "My section includes leadership," says White. "I tell them we want everybody to be a leader. Some people look to managers as leaders, but it's more than that. There's leadership in the household and the community. We want to create an organization of leaders, not 'bosses.'"

Even within an organization that is dedicated to leading through empowerment of employees, there still has to be a hierarchy capped by decision-makers. "Because of employee ownership we have very little turnover in senior positions," says Abtosway. "People below are being mentored for an extended period of time. If someone is ready to move on, someone is ready to move in."

"We are thinking about how we move people up," adds White. "But we're not talking about who the next leader is." Until the day that change comes, White says he has three key goals in leading: "Make sure employees are challenged, rewarded, and having fun. We do reward well, and we do want to have fun doing it. That culture, for me, is important."

● ● ●

Football naturally lends itself to easy analogies about leadership: Quarterbacks are said to command offences and lead teams to a degree not found in any other team sport. But they are helpless without linemen to protect them against the blitz, and they can't put many points on the board without wide receivers, running backs, and kickers. They also can't function without scripted plays, scouting of opposing teams, and game plans. When looking at different leadership models, "captains and sports teams" is one of those eight, being more a blend of scripted and emergent than others. On the one hand, they need to execute set plays; on the other hand, they're highly collaborative with little hierarchy.

If any senior executive in the ranks of Canada's Best Managed Companies would be inclined to offer up a gridiron model for business leadership, it surely would be Gene Dunn, who has seen and experienced leadership from angles few corporate executives experience. He's a past chair of the board of the Winnipeg Blue Bombers (and still serves on its board) and spent seven months as interim commissioner of the CFL in addition to three years as chair of the league's board of governors, from 2006 to 2009. But Dunn offers no wisdom that invokes huddles or hurry-up offence. His one football-related observation arises from the experience of chairing the CFL board of governors.

"The board has sixteen members, and they're all entrepreneurs who are used to leading," he says. Not surprisingly perhaps, in business Dunn prefers a board with a smaller head count. He is one of six members of the board of trustees of the Winnipeg-based Boyd Group Income Fund, which oversees a portfolio of auto body and auto glass service centres in North America. At Monarch Industries, where he is president and CEO, "there are really only four of us on the board." But those four are focused on helping Dunn lead Monarch forward. "Don Streuber, a chartered accountant, and Peter Falk, a lawyer, have been with the board since I arrived," he notes. "They represent an investor and are just outstanding. They've been mentors and provide great experience. They're someone to bounce ideas off. They have been 100 percent supportive in our growth and have played an integral role in our planning." Best Managed Companies also are more apt than others to have an advisory board as part of their leadership structure.

Dunn has been back to university to study marketing and management, but he says his real education in leadership came at Federal Industries. "It was the best education anyone could ask for." Federal Industries was a Winnipeg-based holding company with twenty-six companies organized in four divisions: consumer goods, transportation, steel processing, and distribution. Dunn came out of one of the steel companies, Russel Metals, where he had served for five years, when he assumed the helm of Monarch Industries in 1994. Before that, he had been CEO of Wilson Stationers, which had a chain of one hundred stores, and CEO of Cashway Building Centres. (The year after Dunn left the Russel Metals division, Federal Industries divested itself of its non-metals businesses and became Russel Metals Inc.)

Monarch was making water pumps, systems, and hydraulics when he arrived. "The company wasn't profitable," Dunn says. "It had started in 1935 but had never made a lot of money." The turn-around was so rapid that only a year after Dunn arrived, Monarch was named one of Canada's Best Managed Companies.

After weathering the recent recession, Monarch rebounded with a 30 percent increase in sales in fiscal 2010–11 as it profited from an ambitious multi-year capital-spending program to increase capacity, but more importantly to improve product quality and operational efficiency. The pump division was sold altogether in 2007. The foundry building in Winkler, Manitoba, was expanded, a fully automated paint line was added to the Winnipeg facility, and several new, large items of automated equipment were acquired. A hydraulic assembly facility was also established near Shanghai with a Chinese partner, and while it was aimed at supplying the North

American market, Monarch Industries has been actively researching sales opportunities in Asia, as it considers itself to be the leader in expertise in the hydraulic markets it serves. Its quality assurance is ISO 9001 certified, which is the highest and most comprehensive level and covers the design, manufacture, installation, and servicing of systems.

Companies like Monarch Industries execute three principles of collective leadership: creating a sense of belonging, gaining shared commitment, and achieving a shared interpretation of a problem and the desired solution. Those principles are then applied across the spectrum of capabilities that are needed to drive results: strategy formulation, leadership development, organization design, process design, technology strategy, and change management.

"Our company's success has been achieved through teamwork," Dunn stresses, which is as close as he comes to invoking the world of the Blue Bombers. "A strong leader surrounds himself with talent. I'm a huge believer in succession. Vice-presidents and the people behind them need people who can step up and do their jobs. You need to attract a strong team, and retain it."

A lot of the key people were already at Monarch when Dunn arrived in 1994. Turning the company around required a strategic plan, and to help shape it he hired Roy Cook, who had served in a number of senior management roles in strategic development at Federal Industries. Elevated to COO in 2009, Cook was initially Monarch's director of business development.

Effective leadership is built on communication, Dunn says. Every week, he holds an operations review committee meeting. "Every senior manager sits around a table and discusses the previous week." Quality, customer service, and health and safety get a hearing every week. Sales and marketing might be heard from once every four weeks.

"Every manager is aware of what's going on elsewhere in the company," says Dunn. "It's very open communication. If we've done something wrong with a customer, everyone in the organization knows it."

● ● ●

McCain Foods is one of the largest private companies in Canada and one of the world's most recognized brands. No company on the globe produces more frozen potato products than McCain, which is responsible for about one-third of the world's French fries. Whether they're buying them in a local supermarket or ordering them in a restaurant or a cafeteria, consumers in about 160 countries on every continent, save Antarctica, know McCain's fries. And until very recently, the task of leading that global organization, with production facilities in forty-four countries, was associated with two founding brothers from New Brunswick. But leadership today at McCain is synonymous with transformation—of how it makes it food products (which go well beyond French fries), of how the global company is organized, and in particular how a new idea of leadership is being driven deep into the employee ranks.

In 1909, a New Brunswick farmer, Andrew (A.D.) McCain, diversified beyond growing and selling potatoes locally by creating McCain Produce, a seed export company. His sons developed business ambitions of their own, and in 1957, Wallace and Harrison McCain, supported by two of their brothers, entered the frozen-food business with their first French-fry plant, in Florenceville, New Brunswick. It was the start of an enterprise with global reach in production and $6 billion in annual sales. While potatoes represent the bulk of the company's production, its offerings include frozen pizza, vegetables, appetizers, desserts, and beverages.

Two boards oversee the company. Holdco is the McCain family holding company; Opco (on which three family members hold seats) is the operating company. Wallace McCain passed away in 2004, and when Harrison McCain passed away in May 2011, the company was already embarking on a restructuring of the operating company.

Where McCain previously operated through decentralized operations in different countries, today the company is reorganized around regions under a new global CEO, Dirk Van de Put. McCain Foods (Canada) is now part of a larger regional operation, called the Americas.

That corporate restructuring overlapped with two other initiatives. The first was in its product offerings. In January 2010, the company launched the It's All Good initiative. McCain aligned its offerings with the "real food" movement, striving to use only ingredients consumers could recognize—and pronounce. Launched publicly in January 2010, the company vows: "If you can't find an ingredient in your own kitchen cupboard, then it's our goal to remove it from our products." More than seventy new recipes and new products were introduced in 2010 alone. The company also improved the products nutritionally whenever possible, such as lowering sodium levels. The It's All Good initiative has been aided by the introduction of a world-class research department within McCain Foods (Canada), where there had been no formal research facility at all five years earlier.

The other initiative was the one to drive the idea of leadership deep into the employee ranks, which was no small undertaking in an enterprise that had grown from thirty employees at the original Florenceville plant to more than nineteen thousand around the globe. Three thousand of those employees are with McCain Foods (Canada), working in twelve different locations across the country.

"We had two founders who were dynamic personalities and incredible business people who had an influence on all of the company," says Darryl Rowe, president of McCain Foods (Canada). "For the business to continue to grow and flourish, each employee has to embrace the fact that everybody in the organization has an opportunity to lead. It's an evolution of the culture. It was there before, but we want to encourage people to embrace it."

Modern organizations are complex, with many levels and matrixed dimensions. In a large organization like McCain, the challenges of leading and of fostering a change in the way leadership is viewed and embraced by employees are especially elevated. Companies have to ask if people truly care about the parts of the organization they are being asked to further, and they need to understand where employees' allegiances really lie in the organization. It might be with their team, their office, or their line of business. Are these employees ready to act together to achieve their goals? More to the point, who's really on the bus and committed to taking actions needed to achieve the organization's goals? A dozen aren't nearly enough when an organization needs to engage thousands. Employees need to have the information that will help them to decide whether they are committed or not and to understand the ways in which the organization gets work done. And given the many ways people can work together, there has to be agreement on how people will work together. An executive may decide his or her leadership architecture is "conductor and orchestra," which will produce a lot of sour notes in a workforce that envisions itself as an ensemble of improvisational jazz musicians.

McCain has been striving to foster change in a large, global organization by delivering a consistent message of expectation of empowerment. "We want people to express their views, to say what they think they can do to make a positive contribution," Rowe elaborates. "We're encouraging 'straight talk,' to say what's on their minds, to make us better. Leadership is not an exclusive right of people in senior positions. Leading is something everyone has an opportunity to do."

One of the ways McCain is developing leaders is through its Leaders as Teachers initiative. "It's about how we want to get new learning throughout the organization as quickly as possible," says Rowe. "It also gives people the opportunity to lead core training from within the organization. We look for people who can take a leadership role to bring learning to life."

A prime example of the application of Leaders as Teachers is its role in the implementation of a new information-system platform across North America, which is part of the One McCain technology initiative that began in Great Britain in 2010. The aim over a four-year period is to implement common industry processes across all regions, establish a global IT system built on the new platform, and improve collaboration across regions and work groups

"We've identified 'power users' or 'super users,' who are critical to this implementation," says Rowe. "They exist at all levels of the organization. They're intended to be 'go-to' people who can bring a new system to life. Leaders as Teachers training puts us in a position to do that."

Formalized instruction takes place in three-day training sessions with professional facilitators. "I could be in there getting the same training as a front-line manager," says Rowe. "We don't take it for granted that people can be great teachers unless they've been properly trained."

Rowe says "it's a real exciting time at McCain. We have a new global CEO who is doing a lot to reinforce importance of clear communications with employees across the globe." The process began with a leadership conference in the summer of 2011, attended by senior leaders from McCain operations around the world. The changes were then communicated to McCain Foods (Canada) through a variety of strategies and channels. "We've been using everything from face-to-face meetings to technology," says Rowe. McCain has employed e-mails from the global CEO and regional president, regular postings on the corporate intranet, WebEx presentations by Rowe, employee newsletters, posters, and team meetings at all function levels. "It's a way to engage employees beyond their local responsibility, and for the global company to be relevant locally, where the action happens," says Rowe.

For the face-to-face meetings, Rowe and other senior executives have embarked on "road shows" to Canada's twelve McCain facilities to communicate changes at McCain, and to engage employees in fostering further change. "It's more than just about presenting results," says Rowe. "We're talking to them about where the business is going and the key initiatives we're taking so we can continue to grow."

"We want to clearly communicate results and the priorities of the business," Rowe adds. "But we also want to give people an opportunity to be heard. The most important part of it is to get questions and feedback from employees. We come away with meaningful and tangible things. We get great feedback through a survey after every session that also communicates how to make the sessions better."

● ● ●

The companies in this chapter vary enormously in size, but their essential leadership philosophy is the same. Leaders do more than issue orders. They need to be supported by talent in decision-making, and they are increasingly looking to employees, once considered to be followers, to step into leadership roles themselves. "We give people a chance to be heard," summarizes Darryl Rowe of McCain. "And that goes back to the idea of giving everybody a chance to lead."

Giving people the chance to be heard begins with the management team recognizing that that they deserve to be heard. As Apex Distribution tells its own employees, "the person doing the job knows best." An organization's people can then become empowered with initiative, decision-making, and input into processes, products, and strategy. With that empowerment comes increased accountability for the individual employee, as exemplified by the open-communications meetings at Monarch Industries, where "If we've done something wrong with a customer, everyone in the organization knows it." But that accountability also means greater opportunity for employees in their career trajectory and for the organization overall as a dynamic, profitable entity. In the process, new leaders within the traditional reporting hierarchy can be identified and mentored. Most important, companies think carefully about the kind of leadership that best reflects their culture and business, and embrace and foster this leadership style.

# 3

# BRANDING AND MARKETING: MAKING THE PRODUCT AN EXPERIENCE, NOT A THING

In 1992, Brent Hesje was hired as the new marketing manager at Fountain Tire. He arrived at a growing chain of automotive tire retailers in Western Canada that was far less known than the tires it was selling. Fountain Tire was foremost a Goodyear dealer (Goodyear Canada owns a minority share of Fountain Tire), and brand surveying revealed that while Goodyear had a 98 percent recognition rate, Fountain Tire, which was the overwhelming source of Goodyear tires in the market, was down at 17 percent. Consumers knew *what* they were buying, but didn't really know *where* they were buying it.

Hesje had previously earned a bachelor of commerce from the University of Saskatchewan, but the strength of his perspective on Fountain Tire's challenges lay in his most recent experience as a sales manager at the consumer products giant, Procter & Gamble. "I came to realize when I was with Procter & Gamble, a great branding company, that product was experience," says Hesje, who became Fountain Tire's CEO in 2005. The company was not projecting one of its major assets: the expertise of the chain and the quality of the customer experience.

"I would listen to the advertising that Fountain Tire was running," Hesje recalls. "It was very product based and basically would end with, 'you can go buy this at Fountain Tire.' Signage was also primarily the tire brand." Fountain Tire was a place with poor consumer brand recognition that sold a brand that consumers knew very well. "The majority of the awareness was for Goodyear, not Fountain. I wanted to flip that around."

Fountain Tire's subsequent transformation into a retail enterprise focused on increasing and leveraging the value of its own brand is a textbook case of a trend we have seen among Canada's Best Managed Companies winners. There has been an increasing emphasis on the competitive opportunities of branding and marketing. It wasn't long ago that the big consumer brand companies were the ones predominantly attuned to these priorities, but there has been a discernible shift, with private and/or mid-market companies investing in the time, talent, and processes necessary to move their brands forward.

A brand is much more than a logo, a trademark, or a bottle of pop on a supermarket shelf. Every business is itself a brand, with values to be cultivated, protected, understood by its employees, and communicated to the marketplace. Branding and marketing have thus been elevated from a departmental responsibility within a company to the point of anchoring overall strategic planning. A new generation of smart leaders has begun to grasp the competitive advantage of the "power of the brand" at all enterprise scales, to recognize that this power does not belong solely to major consumer icons like Coke or Apple or Ford. In some cases, they are recognizing the opportunities for brand extension, using the strong attributes of a core brand to expand their business into new avenues.

A brand also is not something that can be papered over by an organization with clever slogans or advertising. It reflects the authentic value of the enterprise to the client. The client's perception of brand must align with the company's self-perception if the brand is to have true value. Companies with strong brands understand that they emerge from within the organization. The brand embodies core values, reflects core competencies, and arises from strategic planning. If it is a mere persona, customers will recognize the brand for the mask it is.

The companies we meet in this chapter illustrate how companies grapple with multiple dimensions of branding and marketing. All but one of them is in the business-to-consumer (B2C) sector. Companies often represent or retail one or more brands that have national or global status, but are themselves brands. They understand that brands leverage other brands and that major consumer brands must deliver value at a local level. And more often than not, a brand that appears to be about a product is in fact (as Brent Hesje of Fountain Tire recognized) about an experience—a promise to their customers. The value to the customer of the brand is reinforced, and even found, at the level of interaction between company and customer. That lesson carries over handily to the business-to-business (B2B) company we profile, Knightsbridge Human Capital Resources, which has thrived by branding itself not as a human resource service, but rather as a "thought leadership" enterprise that aligns its marketing efforts with the experiential by connecting current and potential clients with its own experts.

●  ●  ●

Fountain Tire began in 1956 as a two-bay garage in Wainright, Alberta, a town 200 kilometres southeast of Edmonton. When its founder, Bill Fountain, died in a car accident in 1976, he left behind a chain of nineteen stores and a group of managers and employees who wanted to keep the Fountain Tire name alive and the business growing. Expansion, though, was modest. By 1987, the chain had reached thirty stores in Western Canada. At that point, Goodyear Canada acquired a minority interest, and the chain's growth accelerated.

Fountain Tire now has more than 140 outlets in Canada. Of those, 81 are in Alberta, 38 in British Columbia, 15 in Manitoba, and 10 in Saskatchewan. It also has one in Whitehorse, Yukon, and has expanded into northwestern Ontario, with outlets in Red Lake and Thunder Bay. In 2011, it breached the southern Ontario market with a store in Vaughan, just north of Toronto.

When Brent Hesje arrived in 1992, his desire to make Fountain Tire rather than Goodyear the primary brand did not mean he was in any way wary of Fountain Tire's relationship with Goodyear. The tire manufacturer and minority partner clearly is a major brand asset. "We believe in national brands," says Hesje. "If we put our local flair on it, which ultimately depends on trust, we can be successful." He preaches the virtue of *glocal*—to think globally but act locally.

In addition to illustrating how more companies are recognizing the power of their own brands, Fountain Tire is exemplary of the way an enterprise can capitalize on (and support) a national or global brand like Goodyear at a local level by becoming a strong brand in its own right. It's not enough for a dealer to stock a brand-name product. The product itself is less about a *thing* than an *experience*, and the dealer or distributor provides the consumer with an accompanying experience at the local level that can make or break the value proposition of the national or global brand it represents. It educates consumers about the brand and supports their purchase decisions. It is also the human interface in the transaction, the level at which trust is built and reinforced.

Making Fountain Tire a strong brand in its own right had the additional benefit of extending the brand in a way the retail chain never could if it relied solely on products it sold. By building a Fountain Tire brand around trust and experience, the company could extend the brand more effectively into a wide variety of automotive services. Fountain Tire sells three main tire brands—Goodyear, Dunlop, and Kelly—with product for almost every conceivable market, including consumer cars and trucks, semi-trucks, recreational vehicles, farm and tractor, and industrial and mining sectors. But it also offers a wide range of mechanical services for vehicles: air conditioning, fuel systems, brakes, suspension, steering, exhaust, transmission, belts and hoses, and oil changes, to name a few.

That brand extension, and brand autonomy for Fountain Tire, has become more critical as time has passed. Even with Goodyear acquiring a significant equity stake in Fountain Tire, the retail chain has not retained an exclusive right to Goodyear product. "We're not as exclusive as we were when we started," says Hesje. "Today, consumers can purchase Goodyear products from other retailers." In Edmonton, for example, where Fountain Tire has a strong presence, it must compete directly with mass merchants such as Canadian Tire and Walmart in the Goodyear line. Mass-merchant retailers, says Hesje, "try to commoditize tires. If there wasn't such a need for a high level of expertise, mass merchants would long ago have taken over." That has saved a dedicated chain retailer like Fountain Tire from competing on price alone. "People don't have time to completely understand their vehicles," says Hesje, and tires are one area where people need and seek advice on the bewildering variety of tread designs, dimensions, and seasonal suitability—a variety that continually changes as new products are introduced. This is where local tire shop operators come into their own.

To compete with the big-box outlets, Fountain Tire stores effectively have to be local shops. "Independent tire stores are still the basis of the Canadian tire market," Hesje explains. "To be successful, you have to be worth trusting. The cool thing about our brand, and our brand experience, is that our store managers own 50 percent of their store. And there are no absentee owners. They have to run the store. Eighty percent of the moves we've made to make our company stronger have come from ideas of managers in the field."

Fountain Tire, says Hesje, "is much more about human interaction, the human side of purchasing" than its competitors. "We're big on loyalty programs, and on humour." Fountain has used actor/comedian Thom Sharp ("the bald guy") as its brand persona since 1994. Introduced as Goodyear's public face in 1991, Sharp's performance lit up a Gallup Poll survey on likeability in Canadian advertising. The smarmy yet vulnerable corporate incompetence of Thom's character somehow works in a counterintuitive way for Fountain Tire, a company that stresses trust, reliability, and sound advice. Sharp's persona (he is identified as "Thom" in Fountain's promotional materials) has been effective at extending and sharing brand recognition with Goodyear. His likeability makes consumers want to hear the marketing message he does manage to deliver.

With Thom Sharp, Fountain Tire has successfully deployed a quasi-fictional character as the public face of its brand. Two other Canada's Best Managed Companies winners have long employed their own founders and chief executives as part of their branding and marketing strategies. Both are in the fitness industry; both executives are authors; and both understand how their own personal brand extends to—and interacts with—the brand of their respective companies. And in both cases, brand value, as at Fountain Tire, is all about consumer experience.

● ● ●

"Your brand very much has to be what you are," says David Patchell-Evans, founder and CEO of GoodLife Fitness. "You can't sit down and decide what it's going to be."

David Patchell-Evans is very much a brand in his own right. Everyone knows him simply as "Patch." Both of Patchell-Evans's books draw on his personal narrative as a source of inspiration for readers looking to do more than lose weight or improve their cardio fitness in his chain of fitness clubs.

Patchell-Evans began advertising on television in 1983, developing the brands for both himself and his clubs. "My job was to build credibility in an industry that didn't always have the best reputation. I believed GoodLife had the best product in the fitness space." The company's strategy was "to take a page from the biggest and most successful brand in another industry, in effect adopting what I call 'borrowed branding.'" The company did a spoof on the classic American Express "Do You Know Me?" commercials, putting Patchell-Evans in the ad to promote GoodLife's multi-club membership card and using the memorable Amex tagline "Don't leave home without it."

"I got into fitness by accident, quite literally," Patchell-Evans explains. A motorcycle crash when he was a student landed him in rehabilitation for a lengthy period of time and changed the trajectory of his life. "Rehab taught me so much about how a body works and recovers, and led to a new-found interest in physiology." One week into business studies at university, he decided to switch his academic focus to physical education. Patchell-Evans went on to complete a degree in physical education from Western University. He also became a serious competitive rower and began training at the same fitness club in London, Ontario, as the one used by

Canada's national rowing team. Patchell-Evans ended up taking over the club in 1979, when he was twenty-five; by age thirty-two, he owned seven clubs. Today, GoodLife Fitness has close to three hundred clubs, all of them in Canada. "We are the fourth or fifth largest group of clubs in the world, and we're concentrated in only one country."

David Patchell-Evans is in high demand as a motivational speaker. He draws on his own life experiences to inspire audiences around the world to embrace a fit and healthy lifestyle. Citing his personal challenges, Patchell-Evans explains how he has applied what he has learned from them to help his company grow and to build depth in the values behind the GoodLife brand. "Caring" is one of the company's core brand values, born from two formative experiences beyond the initial motorcycle accident. One was his experience with sudden-onset rheumatoid arthritis. The other was the autism diagnosis of his daughter Kilee.

The arthritis physically overwhelmed Patchell-Evans after returning from a world master's rowing regatta with a haul of medals. "I woke up the next morning with inflammation in my hands and feet and severely limited mobility. I couldn't open a bottle of water. I couldn't pedal on an exercise bike or do the simplest of tasks. What that experience translated into for the company was phenomenal. It taught me that I wasn't indispensible, but that I had a great staff and could rely on them."

Patchell-Evans also stresses that he "learned empathy." From empathy came the brand focus of caring. "Most fitness programs are taught by people who are young, fit, and successful in sports, and I was one of those people. Suddenly, I developed severe arthritis, and I knew what it could feel like to be seventy-five, eighty-five, or ninety-five years old. I started to look at my business differently. Fitness was not about getting strong, but about how you can be the best you can be for your life circumstances. You're not just training for a marathon or the Olympics. It's your body for your entire life. With the members, we say: 'Let's figure out what you need, in order to get the goals or results you want.'" GoodLife has been able to capture that philosophy within its name and communicate it to existing as well as potential clients. Its television advertising has effectively conveyed the message that fitness is achievable for Canadians in all walks of life, and that GoodLife is a place that understands and supports individuals' goals, without holding them up to impossible standards of hyper-athleticism.

Patchell-Evans's personal lessons in empathy continued when his daughter Kilee, now sixteen, was diagnosed with autism at age two-and-a-half. He learned everything he could to help his own and other similarly affected children and families. Patchell-Evans provided the initial funds to establish the Kilee Patchell-Evans Autism Research Group at Western University in 2003. He continues with that commitment and to date has personally donated $4 million to Dr. Derrick MacFabe and his research team of twenty. In 2007, Patchell-Evans received the Canadian Medical Association Medal of Honour for his support of autism research.

During the early years of her diagnosis, Kilee was immersed in a home-based therapy program. "Everyone had to come to the house to meet with me," Patchell-Evans says. It was an abject lesson in the importance of work–life balance for all people, but his daughter's education and therapy also taught him the importance of focusing on an individual's strengths. That lesson fed back into the focus and brand positioning of GoodLife. "We're about what you can do, not what you can't," he says. "We're trying to liberate people. You don't have to be perfect to enjoy a good life."

David Patchell-Evans and GoodLife Fitness have much in common with John Stanton and The Running Room where both target markets and branding are concerned. Stanton was new to running when he launched his company in 1984. He devoted himself to learning the business of retailing sporting goods geared to running with as much gusto as he did to running itself. His first retail space was in a single room of an old Edmonton house, and so the company was called The Running Room. Today, that single room has grown to more than 110 retail outlets in Canada and the United States, as well as an online store. Stanton is the author of two bestselling books on running, and is a widely recognized, approachable face at running events and clinics around North America.

Like Brent Hesje at Fountain Tire, John Stanton has recognized that great brands are built on the consumer's experience, not on *things*. The Running Room ultimately sells *stuff*—running shoes, clothing, and other gear—but as a brand, The Running Room is about doing and, above all, helping people do it.

With Fountain Tire, the key experience is the quality of sales and service an outlet provides to the consumer in retailing quality, brand-name products. For The Running Room, that customer connection at the retail level—a quality experience that informs purchase decisions—is also fundamental. The Running Room has an additional experiential dimension to the brand: engaging the consumer in running in the first place. "We've established a brand around running more than around the retail aspect," Stanton says.

There is some element of this experiential dimension with Fountain Tire as well. Tire purchases are much more of a necessity than a lifestyle choice, but consumers do need to be educated on the need to buy quality, to install a full set of snow tires rather than try to get by on conventional all-season radials, and to service a car regularly. Once they are persuaded that these options are necessities (and a matter of safety to themselves, friends, and family), they are also inclined to take their business to the outlet that educated them and that they feel they can trust.

With The Running Room, as with GoodLife, the lifestyle element is much more front and centre in the relationship between the consumer and the enterprise, although that wasn't always the case. Running has changed, and The Running Room has done much to help change it.

"Running used to be an isolated activity," says Stanton. "We've encouraged the social aspect of it. We've built a sense of community when the world needs more community." Pitching in to build that community and keep it growing is good business practice: "To build market share, the best way is to develop a new market, not just take care of an existing market. It lets you develop a much more loyal customer."

The Running Room can take considerable satisfaction in having built a successful retailing brand based on effecting positive change for customers. One of the key fitness demographics The Running Room has helped create as well as capture is the "born-again athlete"—the individual who at a particular stage of his or her life has decided lacing up shoes and hitting the road or the trails is a needed change, for reasons that often extend well beyond cardiovascular health or body mass index.

"Running has a profound effect on people's lives," says Stanton. "It could be that they want to lose weight, quit smoking, or reduce stress. There could be a divorce, a death in the family, or even a drug addiction they're trying to overcome. It's not only us as a company they turn to. It's the running community they become part of."

One of the keys to having the running community grow has been disengaging it from the purely competitive objective of training. "If you take the intimidation factor of competition away," Stanton says, "running becomes collegial. Ninety percent of our customers are running for reasons other than competition." That doesn't mean runners today aren't attending competitions. But many of them are instead flocking to events that are "runs" rather than races. There may be prizes awarded for top finishing times, but these are typically events in support of charitable causes and can also be mini-vacation getaways with families, friends, or partners. "There are a lot of young moms," says Stanton. "They get to spend time with other women, and they enjoy the camaraderie." In general, he says, running fits the schedule of many women and provides a satisfying social dimension to their lives.

Women in fact have far surpassed men as the most important customer category for his business. Stanton ventures that the customer split by head count is probably sixty–forty female–male, but that the revenue significance is even more skewed. About 70 to 75 percent of purchasing is female driven. Women spend money not only on themselves, but as with household spending in general, purchasing decisions are being made by them for children and male partners. When a couple comes into a store, it's the woman who will tell the man he needs a new pair of running shorts.

To be a successful retailer, The Running Room has long understood that it first and foremost must market the idea of running as a lifestyle—and provide expert advice on how to remain in that lifestyle. Running clinics and clubs get people into the activity and help keep them there in ways that are personally and socially satisfying. "The clinics and clubs provide a sense of community, and the clinics teach people how to take up running relatively injury-free, and allows them to choose their destination."

The Running Room's marketing philosophy is not to encourage people into going shopping. It's to encourage them into running (and walking) and help keep them there. It has created runners who continue to turn to The Running Room for advice, which ultimately leads them to purchase what The Running Room is selling.

Patchell-Evans has similarly built a successful fitness company by recognizing the importance of lifestyle. The concept, indeed, is right in the company name. "Our brand is about translating our passion for fitness into caring for our members the best way we know how," he says. "What is life to you? What is a good life? Our goal is to give every Canadian the opportunity to live a fit and healthy good life." From the beginning, he wanted to differentiate GoodLife from the still-ceaseless TV promises of self-improvement products and services that tell consumers "you can accomplish everything in ten minutes." And as the chain of clubs grew, he also understood better how fitness fit into people's lives, and adjusted the club's offerings and brand positioning accordingly.

GoodLife had come to understand the same socializing preroga-tive of the new generation of runners that The Running Room catered to. "Next to a member's home and business or school, the club is often central to their lives," Patchell-Evans says. "GoodLife members develop social networks that are unique to each and every one of our three hundred clubs. They have their own personality, often driven by those members, of which the staff are an integral part."

People want to congregate at a club, just as they do in The Running Room's running clinics or groups and at 5K charitable runs. "The club is a shared space," says Patchell-Evans. "People need the best equipment and change rooms, but they also need to do their activities together. People are using fitness clubs in general around the world more than they ever have. It's about knowing you're in a space where you have things in common with other people. We're gregarious. We're family oriented and team oriented."

GoodLife is renowned for its group exercise programs, and once the company recognized the socializing aspect of these programs, it stopped calling them "classes" and started calling them "groups." Patchell-Evans also knows that his own qualifications are crucial for brand positioning. "You can trust the company because you can trust the owner." GoodLife Fitness and The Running Room are brands that David Patchell-Evans and John Stanton have built through and around themselves.

● ● ●

Riding a Harley may seem to be a far cry from working out in a fitness group or running in a 5K charity event, but there's more common ground between the branding and marketing of Harley-Davidson motorcycles and that of GoodLife Fitness and The Running Room than many might think.

Deeley Harley-Davidson Canada is the Canadian distributor for Harley-Davidson Inc., one of the most venerable, most *American* consumer brands, with roots in Milwaukee reaching back to 1903. It has become an iconic motorcycle brand allied with the personae of law enforcement and outlaws alike, of easy riders and lone wolves, and it is now beloved by recreational riders from of all walks of life, including more than a few retirees hitting the road together. The company endured about a decade as part of an agglomeration of recreational brands (alongside swimming pools and sailboats) under the AMF umbrella before a management takeover in 1981 "set the eagle free." Since 1986, Harley-Davidson Inc. has been a public company.

Harley-Davidson is a dominant force in the "heavyweight" motorcycle market, which is the domain of machines of 651cc and up. In the United States, the heavyweight category accounts for about 60 percent of new motorcycle registrations; as in Canada, Harley-Davidson holds around 45 percent of the heavyweight market, setting the pace in the cruiser and touring categories. The cruiser category, which the company pioneered, "emphasizes styling and individual owner customization," according to Harley-Davidson. The touring category, which includes three-wheel models, "incorporates features such as saddlebags, fairings, or large luggage compartments and emphasizes rider comfort and load capacity."

Deeley Harley-Davidson Canada has distributed the Harley line exclusively in Canada since 1973 and today has a network of about seventy dealers. It buys Harley-Davidson product at wholesale prices from the U.S. company and sells it in turn to its own dealer network. Deeley has enjoyed a remarkably long run as one of Canada's Best Managed Companies: It was recognized for the seventeenth consecutive year in 2011.

"Traditionally," says Deeley Harley-Davidson Canada president Malcolm Hunter, "our customer was the retailer. But we now look at the whole process. The basis of success is now the exceptional customer experience. We focus on the consumer relationship."

Despite years of acknowledged operational excellence, Deeley Harley-Davidson Canada received "a big wakeup call" with the economic downturn of 2008–09. Hunter freely offers: "We'd talked about the importance of the consumer, but …"

When a recession sideswiped the global economy, the wheels practically fell off the motorcycle market as consumer spending on recreational items in general plummeted. In Canada, a heavyweight motorcycle is generally not a utilitarian vehicle the owner uses to ride to work every day. Sales are driven by the lure of the open road in fair weather, and it wasn't hard for people uncertain about their jobs or the size of their investment portfolio to put off to sunnier economic times a purchasing decision on such a significant discretionary item.

Deeley had increased Canadian Harley-Davidson sales 12 percent between 2007 and 2008, while U.S. sales fell 13 percent. Then the recession hit hard: Canadian sales dropped 30 percent from the company's outstanding 2008 performance, while U.S. sales continued to contract with a further drop of 26 percent. The Canadian downturn was made more painful by what Hunter calls a "perfect storm" of factors. After the high-water sales mark of 2008, Deeley ordered optimistic levels of new inventory. When the market contracted in 2009, Deeley was holding a glut of motorcycles acquired with what had proven to be expensive Canadian funds.

Sales have not recovered to the record levels of 2008, but Deeley Harley-Davidson Canada was able to increase its market share of the heavyweight bikes from 41 to 45 percent in 2011, and the company and its dealers are focused on brand and marketing as never before.

"It used to be that we just took orders," Hunter says, looking back on the early history of the distributorship. The Harley name sold itself. "Not anymore." His company is not so much representing a particular kind of recreational machinery as it is enhancing the consumer's experience of the brand, as represented by both the product and individual dealers. In the process, Deeley is striving to reinforce the historic value of the Harley-Davidson brand while expanding its appeal into new customer groups. "We draw a direct line between customer experience and profitability." Hunter's company wants to understand the customer's experience with the bike they buy as well as with the dealer from whom they buy it.

"Three to four years ago, as long as we paid our bills and had market share, Harley-Davidson left us alone," Hunter explains. "They've woken up to the value of their brand and want to be a world player, and are paying more attention to the position of the brand."

Harley-Davidson says its core U.S. customer base is men over the age of thirty-five and defines its "outreach" customers there as women, young adults, and "ethnically diverse adults." Since 2010, Harley-Davidson has been using an Internet-based crowd-sourcing model to gather guidance from dedicated Harley owners for the direction it takes in defining the brand. Says Hunter: "We're trying to understand how the company is positioning the brand worldwide and how we can customize that definition to meet the Canadian culture, because it's totally different here than in the U.S. We're more culturally diverse right across the country. It's an exciting difference for us."

The average customer age in Canada, Hunter explains, is forty-four, and they are mostly male. "We need to go on outreach. We need to find new customers." Harley owners already are a more diverse bunch than the stereotypical lone wolves of the open road. "We do have the loner of self-expression," Hunter agrees. "But we also have the riders who congregate and socialize." The Harley Owners Group (H.O.G.) in fact has existed since 1983 and provides a formal community, including rallies, for about a million "hog" enthusiasts worldwide. The company has looked to parallel points of congregation—music festivals, martial arts events, among others—to spread the Harley brand message.

There's an intriguing parallel here with The Running Room, which has capitalized on and helped foster a shift in running away from competition-focused loners to a socially motivated community. "We do breast cancer fundraising," says Hunter. "We've done Movember," the annual November charitable fundraiser in which "Mo Bros" grow a moustache in support of prostate cancer education, survivorship, and research. "We've been astounded at how successful Movember has been with the community."

In the case of running, the socially oriented growth of the customer base has come predominantly through women. That isn't happening to the same degree in the Harley world, but more women are riding bikes of their own, as opposed to being a passenger on a man's bike, and they are increasingly riding with other women and not just male partners. Canadian dealers are hosting women-only events under the Garage Party banner. "Women," Hunter says with good humour, "are an interesting group of people we've had to learn a lot about."

As in the United States, Deeley and its Canadian dealers are conducting outreach with youth as well as with competitive riders. "The perception of the competitive rider is we're an arrogant group. We're elitist. We're not welcoming. Our product is too unreliable and expensive. Which is not true, in our view. We're trying to break down barriers and become more inclusive."

As Deeley Harley-Davidson Canada and the American manufacturer look to new demographic segments for the growth they need, they inevitably encounter the hurdle any company faces when they have a venerated brand: resistance to anything new or different from within the longstanding customer core. "Our customers are very loyal, and one of the biggest challenges we have with our core rider is change," Hunter acknowledges. The introduction of liquid cooling to a motorcycle line acoustically branded by its air-cooled engine was an anathema to old-school Harley lovers. "We have bread-and-butter core riders to take care of," Hunter says. The company has to walk the fine line of attracting a new generation of riders with variations in product and not alienating the customer base whose enthusiasm has made Harley-Davidson a truly iconic American brand with a global appeal.

"What's important is the way the marketing program has stayed dynamic," says Hunter. "For us as an organization, it's part of our culture."

● ● ●

Knightsbridge Human Capital Solutions differs from the other companies we've met in this chapter in that it operates in a business-to-business (B2B) rather than a business-to-consumer (B2C) environment. That makes many of its strategies for marketing different, but the essential theories of building, maintaining, and marketing a strong brand are no different.

"The brand building blocks are the same for us," says Leslie Carter, Knightsbridge's vice-president of marketing. "You create a unique product or service, take it to the marketplace, and communicate its value to the customer." Adds David Shaw, Knightsbridge's founder, president, and CEO: "The theory of brand strategy doesn't change in B2B. The tactics do. It's still about understanding customer needs and delivering solutions. How you differentiate yourself may be different."

Knightsbridge offers integrated solutions to companies large and small, public and private, across the full breadth of human capital issues. It was founded by Shaw in July 2001; the company says it was the first consulting company in Canada to be an integrated provider of human capital and talent management solutions.

"Knightsbridge was founded with two crucial differences from traditional human capital management (HCM) consulting firms," the company states. "First, the company believed that creating long-term value for clients and employees meant providing integrated services that meet human capital management needs at every stage in the employment life cycle; from recruitment and selection, to building organizational and leadership capacities, to career management and transition. Second, in order to create value for shareholders investing in the business, Knightsbridge adopted two fundamental goals that had normally opposed each other in HCM consulting: to build a professional services firm known for its quality and people while building a great operating company that measures progress against best-in-market metrics." Through organic growth and acquisitions, Knightsbridge has built a presence in nineteen Canadian cities and has begun expanding beyond Canada.

As Shaw explains, "You're always looking to create a different business model, one that's difficult to replicate. Creating a strong differentiator, that's the magic. It's easy to build a group of services, but I believed consulting was often more product-driven than customer-focused." Knightsbridge says it instead has focused on delivering new ideas and integrated solutions that address their clients' needs. "It's what we've tried to create and it's what the market knows us for."

"We see the brand as a strategic human capital advisor based on three interconnected differentiators," says Carter. "The first is our unique integrated business model. We provide a variety of human capital services, whereas our competitors usually do one thing. Second is the quality of our subject-matter experts. People are our product. What we're offering is their ideas, and clients are getting the best people in the human capital space. The third is culture. Our people have to do what they do well while working collaboratively with others to solve our clients' issues. We're extremely customer-centric and we think that's one of our biggest differentiators."

"One of the things we've tried to bring to this business is that brand actually does matter in B2B," Shaw explains. "We've taken a B2C approach that differentiates us. Competitors are more of what I would call a manufacturing-based business. They sell product. We sell thought leadership. If you can articulate that in a way that has impact on a client's organization, you can be successful."

Whether a business is engaged in B2B or B2C, it is concerned with building credibility with the customer, Carter advises. The difference is in the way that credibility is conveyed. Overall, a typical B2C enterprise is more likely to rely on advertising to build brand identity and credibility, whereas direct interaction with the customer has been the forefront of Knightsbridge's B2B strategy. That has also been the case with some of the B2C companies we have already examined in this chapter, as they have identified *experience* rather than a *thing* as a key differentiator for their brand.

"It's about building relationships, and selling through relationships," says Carter. In B2C, for example, companies often use event sponsorship to build an association of a brand with an activity, both to raise their consumer profile among a desired demographic and to associate with perceived shared values. An auto manufacturer might sponsor a golf tournament to this end. At the same time, a golf club manufacturer might sponsor the same tournament, seeking a more direct association between its product and the activity.

In the B2B environment, Knightsbridge is careful to avoid this sort of marketing of their brand, even when it might seem logical to associate the company with an event that appears specifically associated with some aspect of its basket of expertise. "I would never sponsor a conference that focused on one aspect of the services we provide, such as executive search or career transition, for example," says Carter. The focus is too narrow, too "product" based. "Competitors are transactional or product oriented," she says. "We're going to rise above that, and look at a client's challenges more broadly, from a different perspective. In manufacturing, people enable the product. In our case, people *are* the product."

Knightsbridge continues to market its brand through its "K" campaign, with the single capital letter accompanied by the slogan "Stronger people, stronger organization." At the same time, the company has increased its use of strategic sponsorships, where the aim is to share its expertise and practical experience. Event sponsorship can accomplish that, but only if the actual event allows Knightsbridge to showcase its people and demonstrate their capabilities. An event must also allow Knightsbridge to nurture relationships with existing clients and reach out to prospective ones. Knightsbridge takes clients to events so that they can benefit from them and have the value of Knightsbridge's service reinforced. To that end, Knightsbridge has found success as lead sponsor of the Art of Leadership Conference. Knightsbridge also seeks opportunities to communicate its expertise and experience through partnerships that target its senior-executive audience. Its work producing research with the Institute of Corporate Directors has been greatly beneficial to that end.

Knightsbridge uses its *onPeople* e-newsletter, which is now distributed to more than fifteen thousand clients monthly, to constantly communicate its capabilities through articles and research. Knightsbridge says the newsletter enjoys "open" and "click-through" rates above B2B industry norms.

An important difference between Knightsbridge and the B2C companies we have met in this chapter is the way they approach social media. Companies are turning to Facebook in interacting with consumers, whereas Knightsbridge instead uses LinkedIn to focus on networks of professionals.

For all companies, social media is an indispensible, even unavoidable, aspect of branding and marketing. Consumers are empowered as never before by free Internet applications like Twitter and Facebook. They can communicate likes and grievances around the world. It has long been true that with mature, iconic brands, consumers can feel that the brand belongs as much to them as it does to the holder of the trademarks. Today, the value of all brands to some degree is in the hands of the consumer or the client.

Companies have learned that Facebook in particular presents a communications opportunity much different from a mailing list or even a corporate website. Facebook may be organized in pages, but it functions as a forum for all users, and users who "like" a particular page or "friend" aren't necessarily always friendly. Companies accustomed to having customer complaints handled internally can find their Facebook page overflowing with unflattering allegations. While abusive content and visitors can be blocked, a surprising number of companies have embraced the rough-and-tumble opinions and exchanges of this leading social medium.

The Running Room has been on the Internet practically since there was an Internet. Where Facebook is concerned, the company has crafted two distinct but conjoined presences—one for the store chain and another for John Stanton. And while it has an online shopping presence, most sales still happen in a bricks-and-mortar store.

"The Web has always been a branding tool," says Stanton. "The information we present is about running, not about The Running Room. Our Web presence is primarily to promote running and to drive people into The Running Room Stores." The store is where customers satisfy their needs for fit-function-feel. "The knowledge they get in the store is also important. The person talking to them is a runner. The customer understands, 'This guy or gal really knows what they're talking about.'" It's a brand differentiator the Fountain Tire managers, up against big-box retail outlets in selling snow tires, well understand.

Fountain Tire for its part has made effective use of the Internet. In addition to information deployed through its corporate website, it uses YouTube to post its popular content featuring spokesperson

Thom Sharp. Fountain Tire has extended the use of Sharp to video road trips that have included in-character interviews with members of the Vancouver Canucks.

GoodLife Fitness has a comprehensive social media platform that members and non-members visit for a variety of reasons, including connecting with other members, a club team, accessing information on schedules, and club activities. Facebook, Twitter, and YouTube all have an important place in member engagement.

The Internet is not where the average Harley owner has been thought to hang out, but social media has proved to be far more important to engaging current and prospective owners than almost anyone would have predicted. Garage Party events for female riders are promoted through the website. The Harley Owners Group (H.O.G.) members can now access information on owner events and promotions through the Web with a password-protected membership. "We need to be there," Malcolm Hunter says of the Internet. "We're fast-forwarding that. And we're there."

● ● ●

When asked about Knightsbridge Human Capital Solutions' branding objective, Leslie Carter reiterates: "It's all about building credibility and relationships. Our people create both, but it's marketing's job to promote that credibility and enable the development of relationships. A B2B company does sell to another company, but it does so to people in a company that have issues and challenges to solve. Professional services typically sell something, and they can go in to see a client thinking they're going to sell product A or B. But sometimes what we sell has to be created. Our approach is to give a general understanding of what we do, listen to the client, and then figure out how we can help them." The Knightsbridge model is for the enterprise to be greater than the sum of its parts, to be more than a hive of individuals with specific skill sets linked to particular products.

"You amplify the expertise in the organization," says Carter. "You bottle it and export it to the marketplace." Adds David Shaw: "You have to recognize that a client, which is people or a team, has a challenge. The glue here is that we have the best team that can be put against that challenge."

Knightsbridge's brand in other words is not about a *thing*, any more than The Running Room is about shoes, or GoodLife Fitness is about elliptical trainers, or Fountain Tire is about snow tires, or Harley-Davidson is about a specific motorcycle. They have all built brand excellence upon and crafted a supportive marketing message around the experience the customer can expect from the enterprise, and they all know that brand value rests in the perceptions and loyalties of those customers. Specific products change. The differentiator for these brands is the client's faith in their competency, an adaptable expertise that can find solutions to their needs. That adaptability in turn makes a brand capable of extending in whatever direction opportunity presents. It can go where the customers' evolving needs are, not simply where a fixed product or service can be sold.

# 4

# GLOBALIZATION: FACING DOWN THE MONSTERS AND MINING THE OPPORTUNITIES

When *Monsters Inc. 2* is released by Disney Pixar on November 2, 2012, fans of the long-awaited sequel to the 2001 animated hit (which grossed more than US$500 million globally) will at last be revisited by John Goodman's James P. "Sulley" Sullivan, Billy Crystal's Mike Wazowski, and the other scarifying denizens of Monstropolis. Helping turn *Monsters Inc. 2* into a planetary entertainment phenomenon will be Toronto's Spin Master, which has secured the global licence for associated toy products. It's a huge leap forward in brand partnering for the company founded by three friends at Western University in 1994.

The start-up partners had a hit on their hands when they began selling the Earth Buddy, a Chia Pet–like novelty consisting of a head covered in pantyhose material filled with grass seed that sprouted when watered. It was, as the company says, something of a Pet Rock phenomenon. While it hardly seemed the basis on which to build a global enterprise, Earth Buddy in fact demonstrated the three partners' ability to turn novelty into sales successes, to know almost instinctively what will find a consumer following. All three partners are still in the business. Ronnen Harary is chair and co-CEO, Anton Rabie is president and co-CEO, and Ben Varardi is executive vice-president. They're no longer stretching pantyhose filled with grass seed over clay heads. Instead, they're running one of the world's most dynamic children's entertainment companies, built on a foundation of toys.

Holding the global licence for *Monsters Inc. 2* is a great leap forward not only from their Earth Buddy days: It represents a significant step for the company from where it was a half-dozen years ago, when it was already a success with a growing global presence. While that presence was growing, it hadn't yet grown enough for Spin Master to play at the *Monsters Inc.* tie-in level.

"We were strong in North America," says Harary, "but not strong enough in other markets. When you pitch for a global master toy licence, you need to be strong everywhere." For the last few years, building global strength has been Spin Master's driving principle.

● ● ●

Canada's Best Managed Companies are rapidly becoming more global in operations and outlook, to a degree we did not see twenty years ago. They are thinking globally in where they seek sales, establish operations, conduct manufacturing, and source talent and innovation. This accelerating focus on global activity is both opportunistic and defensive. For many Canadian companies that first stepped outside this nation's border to do business with our largest trading partner—and there have been many more of these among the Best Managed Companies in recent years—globalization is a hedge against being overly reliant on the U.S. market. The rest of the world represents opportunity as well as defensive diversification. In the course of reducing exposure to uncertainties in the U.S.

market, some of the Best Managed Companies winners have been buying U.S. companies and using them as a platform to reach South American markets, which is part and parcel of a trend among them to look to the BRIC countries—Brazil, Russia, India, and China— for growth.

In Chapter 10, "Attracting and Retaining Talent: Building the Lattice," we discuss how top companies are now regarding the global labour market as a talent resource. These hirings are locally important while contributing to the competitiveness of the company around the world. In Chapter 5, "Funding Growth: Raising Capital and Pulling the Value Levers," we touch on the importance of demonstrating global competitiveness or potential for Canadian companies seeking fresh injections of private equity. We have also seen companies move manufacturing overseas to take advantage of cheaper labour, but in this latest iteration of global-ization, top companies are expanding into overseas production to service those distant markets, not simply to manufacture items less expensively and ship them back to North America.

In this chapter, we meet three companies in different stages of global activity. Saskatchewan Minerals drew on the confidence and enhanced reputation delivered by its Best Managed status to move onto the international scene in mining operations for the first time. Evans Consoles began an aggressive move into the U.S. market in 2006 as it also rapidly turned to global opportunities. And Spin Master has been taking its established global strategy to a new level in all aspects of its business.

•  •  •

In 2006, Spin Master began to overhaul its business processes, using integrated IT tools to track and analyze data throughout its supply chain. As a result, the company now can proactively manage individual products at specific retailers in a real-time context around the world. This commitment of $20 million in spending coincided with one of the toy industry's greatest global successes: Spin Master's launch of Bakugan.

Bakugan was developed with partners including Sega Toy of Japan and Toronto animation studio Nelvana; Spin Master also became a co-producer with Nelvana as it entered the animation business through Spin Master Studios. Bakugan is a game played with cards and spring-loaded plastic marbles that pop open into warrior creature figurines (*bakugan* is Japanese for exploding spheres), and has a back story of a Bakugan world and human "battle brawlers" who possess the Bakugan warrior-creature balls.

The average adult may be hard-pressed to grasp this. The main thing to understand is that Bakugan was (and continues to be) a phenomenal success. Introduced to Canada in 2007, the game entered the U.S. market in 2008. So popular did it become that by the 2008 Christmas season one Bakugan product was being sold every 2.5 seconds. The Toy Industry Association of America named Bakugan its Toy of the Year of 2009. There were McDonald's Happy Meal tie-ins. In April 2010, *The Simpsons* aired an episode in which Bart became obsessed with a game called "Battle Ball" that was a clear parody of Bakugan.

Bakugan is at once a card game, an animated adventure television series, a collection of figurines, a global online game environment, and a console video game. Two hundred episodes of the television program have been produced for four seasons. "It's shown everywhere from Russia to Mexico to Korea to Taiwan," says Harary. (Teletoon carries it in Canada.) "We really created not only a global toy, but also an intellectual property kids know by name. From a global perspective, we'd never done that before."

Since launching Bakugan, Spin Master has introduced another card-based warrior game, Redakai, whose product universe includes a television show (co-produced with Zodiak Kids of France's Marathon Group), a comic book, and an online community.

Spin Master would not have been able to keep pace with Bakugan's runaway success without its determination to stiffen the IT backbone and improve the company's presence globally. Its enhancements in recent years have allowed Spin Master to avoid a common failing of companies that are already operating internationally. Rather than take a holistic view in the design and expansion of their global networks—the complex web of suppliers, production and R&D facilities, distribution centres, sales subsidiaries, channel partners, and customers, and the flows of goods, services, information, and finance that link them—most global manufacturers focus on fixing individual pieces of the network. The result is suboptimal improvements, wasted efforts, and lacklustre performance. Deloitte's research has shown in particular that supply-chain cost structure has languished in last place among major competitive capabilities in all the industries we have studied. Most companies have been struggling to compete on cost, quality, customer service, and innovative offerings against manufacturers that constantly redesign their businesses from a global point of view. When companies fall behind on network optimization, they're further punished by the immense costs they face in catching up. This often requires them to sell factories, brands, and subsidiaries to competitors at bargain prices, to reduce staff (and lose experienced personnel), and to restructure business processes and information systems.

Back in 2006, Spin Master had offices in the United Kingdom and France, in addition to Los Angeles, but was otherwise reliant on distributors. "The distributors were more transactional," says

Harary. "They weren't getting our products the exposure they needed. They weren't building and sustaining brand for us. So we started chipping away at key countries with our own offices." Mexico was opened three years ago, and Germany, the Benelux countries, and Italy followed. The company now operates a single distribution network for all of Europe.

Spin Master's success depends on launching new products quickly and then maximizing opportunity by monitoring productivity in servicing the retail level. It manages a demand-driven supply chain in a dynamic consumer products retail marketplace. "Lean" is a critical quality of a supply chain that must respond to the fast-paced demands of retailers and consumers on an international scale.

Spin Master has built a direct electronic connection to key customers globally, on a single system. It collects key information daily from retailers, such as the point-of-sale information for the prior twenty-four hours for individual products, as well as the retail in-stock levels and sell-through rates. The system allows Spin Master to assess momentum on each brand and stock-keeping unit (SKU), by retailer, region, and country. With this level of current information in its analytics environment, Spin Master can monitor retail performance at a highly granular level and take immediate action: obtaining additional supply, reducing supply, or implementing additional marketing promotional initiatives. It reviews and takes action on the basis of these market dynamics on a daily basis.

Spin Master's analytics environment delivers full global visibility to the inventory in the entire supply chain and connects the demand side of retailing directly to the supply-side management in its Asia organization. The company can thus effectively manage SKUs that are selling like hotcakes or slow down inventories that are not selling strongly. It can position inventories optimally in the supply channel, whether they are in a factory in Asia or a domestic warehouse; it can also manufacture high-demand product on short lead times. With this level of supply-chain visibility on a global scale, Spin Master can maximize its margins by ensuring the greatest productivity at retail.

By managing a dynamic supply/demand environment on a global level with world-class IT, Spin Master has been able to pursue opportunistic revenue growth while expanding margins. Inventory levels have been reduced by 40 percent, and on a comparative basis it says those levels are 50 percent less per dollar of revenue than other companies in its sector. Because the supply chain is very lean, the company has substantially reduced the need to discount product.

Spin Master says on-time delivery with retailers is in a consistent range of 95 to 98 percent. Its forecast accuracy of consumer demand is about 70 percent, which it says is at world-class levels for its industry. Development time for new products has been shortened by about 25 percent, which has allowed it to increase the breadth of its brands within the same development cycle. Retailers are happy because the company is always in stock with the hottest product available at the right time. Most important perhaps is the way the system has allowed Spin Master to compete globally without succumbing to gigantism. Despite being a much larger company now, it has been able to protect its treasured ability to behave nimbly, as if it's still that brash start-up being run by three guys at university.

● ● ●

Ronnen Harary of Spin Master advises that going global requires patience. "You've got to grow at a nice, steady pace," he says. "If you grow too fast, the core of your business gets hollowed out. Companies thinking about going global need to look at globalization over a very long period of time, unless there's something special about the business."

Greg Smith, CEO of Evans Consoles of Calgary, also counsels patience. "Don't think you can go and in two trips have orders. It's a long process of developing dealers and customer relationships. It's not unusual to see twelve to twenty-four months pass before an order results." He calls it "an investment in faith," which means having faith that the time, money, and human resources required in seeking new business internationally will pay off in good time. "It does make it harder for smaller Canadian companies," he allows. "We can make investments that other Canadian companies hesitate about."

Before patience, though, comes preparation. "We did the research into future markets showing growth," says Smith. "Then we had to take what we do internationally. We needed to go where the infrastructure was rapidly developing." The company identified niches in which its specialized, high-end products could compete, and which featured clients whose needs meant they would pay for premium installations.

Founded in 1980, Evans Consoles is a private Canadian company with its headquarters in Calgary, owned by CEO Greg Smith and chair of the board Bill Burkett. With over 8800 installations worldwide and more than 300 employees, it is the recognized world leader in the design and manufacture of custom control-room solutions for mission-critical and other technology-intensive environments. Its client list ranges widely, from small municipal facilities to major government agencies and Fortune 500 companies. You can find its solutions in major airports, at Boeing, the Pentagon, Microsoft, Google, Deutsche Telekom, Shanghai Power, and Chase Manhattan Bank, to name a few.

Evans products begin where standard office furniture ends—custom-designed to meet each client specification, with steel framing, lifetime warranties, and the required information technology stylishly integrated. Considerable attention is paid to ergonomics, as a well-designed control-room environment promotes better blood circulation and reduction of stresses caused by static postures. Greater operator comfort means an improved ability to concentrate, which is no small consideration in environments where command-centre decisions can mean life and death to others.

"We had an excellent reputation in North America, in industrial and commercial markets," says Smith of the company's stature when he arrived in 2004. Already, back in 1994, Evans Consoles had supplied NASA with the mission control room in Houston for the shuttle program. In 2005, it completed the Shuttle Launch Control Center at Cape Kennedy, for which it received the United Space Alliance's 2006 SFA Supplier Award for its design and ongoing support.

In 2006, Greg Smith led a new focus in the United States, on government agencies with technology needs. Evans Consoles established a showroom in Washington, DC, and hired former military and federal agency employees. "It allowed us to develop much stronger penetration in areas like Defense and Homeland Security," says Smith. The company engaged the U.S. Department of Defense, architects, and large system integrators in making its case for contracts. The methodical beachhead established in Washington, combined with expertise deployed at the local level of potential projects, paid off. The company's sales in this channel went from nil in 2006 to US$10 million in 2008 as Evans Consoles secured more than fifty military and security contracts. An essential part of its U.S. strategy was addressing the needs of the Defense Base Closure and Realignment (BRAC) Commission, whose 2005 report outlined a major overhaul of military base assets. The list of bases ran to twenty-eight pages. Contract sites secured by Evans Consoles included Fort Hood in Texas, Hulbert Air Force Base and McDill Air Force Base in Florida, U.S. Army Corp of Engineers in Alabama, and the State Department in Washington, D.C.

Even while Evans Consoles was securing new business in the United States, it was elevating its efforts elsewhere. China was targeted in 2007. "We've been doing showpiece projects in China for ten or eleven years," says Smith. "We also wanted to do mid-market projects, and for that we needed manufacturing there."

The company secured the expertise of the Howard Balloch Group, a private investment advisory and merchant banking firm based in Beijing that was founded by Canada's ambassador to China from 1996 to 2001. Evans Consoles decided to embark on a "green-field" development rather than partner with a Chinese company, in order to protect its intellectual property. The first plant opened in Kunshan in 2007 and has been joined by another facility in the same industrial park, employing a total of seventy-five. Some standardized components there are shipped back to North America, but the facilities otherwise service the Chinese and Asia markets.

Elsewhere, Evans Consoles expanded its presence with sales offices or showrooms. Through European partners, the company has showrooms in Germany, the Czech Republic, Russia, and Belgium. There are also now three partner showrooms in the Middle East, two in India, and one in South Africa.

Evans Consoles also diversified into airport check-in counters and signage with a new division, Evans Airport Solutions, in 2011 by making two acquisitions. "We had been doing air traffic control towers and radar centres for twenty years," says Smith. "A contractor said, 'Why don't you do check-in counters?' There has been phenomenal growth in airport development and refurbishment globally."

Its efforts in the aviation sector were capped in September 2011 by its coveted IDIQ contract with the U.S. Federal Aviation Administration (FAA). Its supplier status of "indefinite delivery, indefinite quantity" grants Evans Console a favoured position in the FAA regimen normally reserved for large companies like Raytheon. The contract is a prime example of investment and patience paying off. "We were willing to make the investment in technology and the engineering team, in building out the Chicago O'Hare tower over a period of one and a half years." The O'Hare project earned Evans Consoles its IDIQ contract, which means that any airport in the FAA system can pull up a check sheet and order a custom air traffic control tower console solution. The total value of the IDIQ contract, which has a one-year base and two one-year options, could reach over US$9 million if the FAA exercises all of its options. "This was a big win," says Smith. "There was a lot of up-front investment and good faith that there would be opportunities down the road."

● ● ●

If you buy powdered laundry or dishwater detergent or carpet deodorizer, you're a regular consumer of what Saskatchewan Minerals produces: a salt called sodium sulphate.

"We're probably half of the box," says CEO Rod McCann. The 99-percent-pure white powder Saskatchewan Minerals mines and processes at Chaplin in southwestern Saskatchewan is what is known as detergent-grade sodium sulphate. It has a variety of uses, mainly as a carrying agent and a pH balancer that neutralizes certain processes. The pulp and paper industry uses it in whitening liquors. It's also employed in the manufacture of glass, textiles, starch, and livestock mineral feed.

Saskatchewan Minerals began as a provincial Crown corporation in 1948. Over the years it acquired a number of other producers, but eventually got out of the low-grade "salt cake" market to focus on the detergent-grade form at Chaplin. The company was privatized in 1988; Toronto-based Goldcorp sold it in November 2005 to Aristos Capital Corporation, a private venture-capital company based in Calgary. Aristos had been exploring technologies employing sodium sulphate and was investigating raw mineral sources when it learned Saskatchewan Minerals was for sale.

At its peak, sodium sulphate mining was producing 500,000 to 600,000 metric tonnes annually in Saskatchewan. Today, with the focus on high-grade salt, production averages around 120,000 to 150,000 metric tonnes. "It's been a very consistent and lucrative kind of mining, without a lot of peaks and valleys in volume," says Rod McCann, who arrived with the Aristos acquisition. "It's also been very stable in contribution to the workforce and tax base."

The Chaplin facility has about eighty customers, but the main ones are large consumer-brand corporations like Procter & Gamble and S.C. Johnson. Saskatchewan Minerals appeared destined to continue as a steady-as-she-goes producer of a local resource for the North American market, which consumes about 750,000 metric tonnes a year. "When you're producing a bulk commodity that doesn't have a high value, you don't have much opportunity to look beyond the Canadian and U.S. borders to move your product," says McCann. "And when you're tied to your resource base, you can't pick up and move a production facility. There hadn't been a new production facility built in nearly fifty years in North and South America."

Saskatchewan Minerals thus seemed one of the least likely Canadian corporate candidates to embrace the challenges and opportunities of globalization. What changed for the company was that it became fully aware of its core competencies and learned how to formally recognize and then act upon them well beyond Canada's borders.

The first step in that process of self-awareness was becoming ISO 9001:2008 certified in 2008. The second step was being recognized in 2009 as one of Canada's Best Managed Companies. "We were that company that just did things," says McCann. "We knew we were well run. We had great systems in place. But the Best Managed program caused us to identify core competencies and expose weak points, such as internal communication and communication back to our customers. The program has absolutely changed the way we manage our company."

When the company was awarded the Best Managed designation for the first time in 2009, "I saw an absolute shift in the mentality of the organization," says McCann. "We'd had ideas before. Staff would nod their heads in agreement, but we had always been doing things out of one place and we were comfortable with that. Now I was getting pressure from below: 'Let's go.'"

Initially an internal badge of honour, the award created international exposure that attracted partnering opportunities. Around the time of the 2009 award, one of the company's customers approached it about a sodium sulphate deposit in northern Mexico. "They said to us, 'We believe Saskatchewan Minerals can take this from an undeveloped desert outcropping to a full mining operation.'" Soon after the award was announced, opportunity came knocking in the form of Belgium's Manuchar International, a global distributor of chemicals and bulk materials, and the world's largest distributor of sodium sulphate.

In the 1990s, Manuchar began changing from a company focused on commodity trading to one that develops long-term agreements with partners, using financing and innovation in logistics and commodities sourcing to drive its business. Manuchar approached Saskatchewan Minerals to develop the Mexican mine and processing facility because of the international reputation of its existing production, its ISO 9001 designation, and its recognition under the Best Managed program. "It's funny that a small Saskatchewan company is now partnering with a Belgian corporation to develop a mine in Mexico to supply the Latin American markets," says McCann. "It's the beginning of a long-term relationship that we believe can extend to other markets with new ventures."

Saskatchewan Minerals' new global outlook doesn't end with the Mexican mine. Beyond further projects it expects to develop with Manuchar, it is working with European manufacturers and engineers to provide commercial proposals and performance guarantees for its proprietary sodium hydroxide production technology, which uses sodium sulphate as a key raw material.

The company has also become far more attentive to the impact of foreign exchange on its profitability. "We've changed the flow of where our product ends up," says McCann. "We look to increasing and decreasing exports on a quarterly basis, based on the dollar." The company is also now looking at the supply side of its operations, which it had not really done before, in being more strategically aware of foreign exchange impact.

"We spent a year as an organization questioning and positioning ourselves to apply for the Best Managed Companies program," says McCann. "Through that process, we identified a management expertise, and we gained confidence as we reviewed our operations." Mexico is a challenging project. The mine is very remote, 260 kilometres from the processing site and about 2500 to 3000 kilometres from most of Saskatchewan Minerals' current end customers. But now that it has embraced the challenge, Saskatchewan Minerals can envision itself not just exporting to foreign markets, but producing in them as well. Mexico, Spain, and China are all places where it now foresees developing mine operations.

• • •

Saskatchewan Minerals' venture into global opportunities through a partnership with Manuchar is a common theme among Canadian companies. Whether with formal ventures or advantageous alliances, companies have been stepping onto the world stage by employing strategic alignments. Spin Master has long worked with other enterprises to create multifaceted new properties. "We have three new properties coming in 2013, all with partnerships," says Ronnen Harary. Evans Consoles has leveraged its association with companies like General Electric, Siemens, and Raytheon, which provide the technology components of its installations. "We've established relationships with large international companies, and we service their needs," says Greg Smith. "We can also service what we sell." Following customers into the global marketplace is another common theme we have seen among Canadian companies venturing beyond our borders.

Canadian companies are also looking to the global market to diversify their revenue stream and growth opportunities, deleveraging a typical reliance on the U.S. market for exports. "We used to get 80 percent of our sales from the U.S. That's now 50 percent," says Spin Master's Harary. When Saskatchewan Minerals' Mexican venture becomes operational in 2013, its 200,000 metric tonnes of production will eclipse the output of its Chaplin site, and it will send the production to Latin America, not to Saskatchewan Minerals' established North American market.

Harary stresses the benefit of globalization to Canadian

companies in realizing fresh intellectual capital. "You can garner a lot more ideas, especially from the creativity side, with a global presence."

Spin Master also established innovation centres around the world to find and develop the next Bakugan, whatever it might be. In the past, it had relied on periodic visits to important toy-development markets and brokers for inventors. "In Japan, we have local people on the ground now, and they can access a deep network of toy inventors, fifty to sixty of them. We're not coming in twice a year anymore." It's been an opportune time for the company to increase its presence there. "There's a stagnant economy in Japan, with an aging population," says Harary. "Toy people there are thinking internationally." Another innovation centre operates in Toronto, primarily devoted to the Air Hogs toys that really made Spin Master's reputation after the oddball success of the Earth Buddy. Other innovation centres are in Hong Kong, China, and Los Angeles.

"'Mixing the cultures' is the biggest thing for us, from a new product development perspective," says Harary. "We put together a world-class team of individuals that really know this space. The toy business is still partly art. We then manage the nuances of the business with strong backbone systems."

Greg Smith advises Canadian companies looking to increase their global presence to think locally, which includes finding talent there. "When I go to the U.S., I carry U.S. business cards, and I hire American ex-military. We hire local talent, and we play the local way. In China, we have a Chinese plant manager. In fact the only Canadian working there is someone from Calgary who can speak the language."

Ultimately, Canadian companies wishing to move into a global environment have to hone their core competencies. In the case of Saskatchewan Minerals, to a large degree those competencies already existed, but weren't recognized until they documented their ISO 9001:2008 status and devoted the time and resources to earning Best Managed recognition.

"We initially wouldn't have had the belief in ourselves to take on the Mexico project, or the confidence to partner with a company like Manuchar," says McCann. "We weren't utilizing our core strengths. We've realized we're unique, not a sleepy company up in Canada."

# FUNDING GROWTH: RAISING CAPITAL AND PULLING THE VALUE LEVERS

As a salesman in the transportation industry, Doug Tozer found a niche in intermodal rail in the 1970s, a relatively new mode that combined door-to-door trailer with rail service. Capitalizing on his experience as an early adaptor of what is now called non-asset third-party transportation management, in 1988 Tozer (CEO and chair of the board) teamed up with Denise Messier (vice-president of administration and human resources) and Bob Procyk (now retired) to found Wheels International Freight Systems, the core business of what became the Wheels Group.

"Doug Tozer is an entrepreneurial spirit, an innovative spirit," says COO Peter Jamieson, who joined the Wheels Group in the mid-1990s from Dow Chemical. "When he started his own company, others followed him. They were very people-centric and wanted their own company with that kind of family culture. As people followed him, they brought more people, more experience and relationships with them."

For more than twenty years, the Wheels Group was able to grow organically at a robust 25 percent rate per annum. The company became a centre of transportation excellence in North

American shipping. In 2001, it was the first third-party logistics (3PL) company to become ISO-certified.

"Our big difference is that 'asset' players are unable to provide a full multi-mode North American solution," Jamieson explains. Unlike Canada, which is serviced by national railways, the American rail transportation is a warren of regional players. A 3PL like the Wheels Group can enable the most cost-effective mode, equipment, and routing for a client's goods, be it by rail, truck, or ship, or some combination thereof—cross border, anywhere in North America and around the globe.

Staying clear of assets, it focused on services that improved the customers' own supply chain efficiencies. "We created a business intelligence–supply chain solutions team," says Jamieson. "We can analyze, implement, manage, and measure how to optimize a client's supply chain, which differentiated us from the competition. Where do you use rail, road, or a forty-foot marine box? We provide customized reporting online for the customer, in business language the customer understands. We get very granular."

Until 2006, the Wheels Group was satisfied to continue to grow organically. "The company was funded through its own cash flow," says Jamieson. "There was no bank debt." That changed when a prime acquisition became available: the Clipper Group of Chicago, a 3PL founded in 1938 with many like and complimentary services. For the US$120 million acquisition, the Wheels Group turned to a bank for the first time. "In 2006," says Jamieson, "banks were lined up to give you money." The Wheels Group borrowed about $25 million on a five-year term.

A year later, the signs of the recession, the worst since the Great Depression of the 1930s, began to gather. The Wheels Group had been through other recessions, but this one was the first it would face with significant bank debt and an implosion in consumer spending that bit hard into its clients' shipping needs. The company suddenly needed a survival strategy and a model other than bank borrowing to fund its growth, if and when the economy managed to turn the corner on the downturn that the Wheels Group began to feel most acutely in 2008.

● ● ●

Canada's private companies have traditionally funded their growth through three means: cash flow from their own balance sheets, bank borrowing, and injections of capital through management (and friends of management), private equity, and public markets. Canada's Best Managed Companies demonstrate the importance of having access to various sources of financing in order to remain competitive and of scaling their finance departments appropriately as they grow. The Wheels Group saga encapsulates every one of those strategies. In its case, the decision to borrow from a bank to fund its continued growth through a strategic acquisition was almost its undoing.

The Wheels Group started to see the economy softening in the second half of 2007. As a transportation logistics provider, its own business was like a canary in the coal mine of the coming recession. "We tend to be a barometer of economic activity," says Peter Jamieson. Companies in the food industry had outsourced their shipping requirement to the Wheels Group, and while that helped with the company's customer diversification, it also gave Wheels a front-row view of declining consumer spending.

More worrying was the retraction in the automotive industry that began to emerge in 2008. Here, the Wheels Group was particularly exposed through its IWheels Dedicated Logistics division, which it had started in 2001. The division had grown to a $75 million revenue generator by 2007, but it was focused on the automotive/OEM (original equipment manufacturer) sector in Ontario, becoming the leading transportation supplier to GM in Oshawa and Ford in Oakville and St. Thomas. It was the Wheels Group's only "asset" operation. "It was a light-asset model, as it used owner-operators," says Jamieson. "But we had a lot of liability through trailer leases and inconsistent revenues." As the automotive industry bore some of the worst impacts of the recession, the Wheels Group tried to keep pace by reducing expenses. But it was a losing battle. "You couldn't cut costs fast enough."

"For the first time we had bank debt and had stepped into a recession with high exposure to automotive/OEM," Jamieson recalls. "That was quite a challenge to deal with. We really scrambled through mid-2008 to 2009."

It's in the day-to-day operations, reflected in the balance sheet, that companies have been finding the funds to fuel their growth and the operational intelligence to accurately forecast future cash flows and capital requirements, a critical capability whether business is growing or retreating.

● ● ●

When John Gleason joined 4Refuel in January 2011 as its new CEO, the company was about six months into a new line-of-credit arrangement with TorQuest Partners, one of Canada's top private equity firms, which had been negotiated to help it expand in the United States and Europe. The line of credit was left untapped as expansion outside of Canada was put on hold. 4Refuel had found enough growth opportunities within Canada to set aside international plans. It had also found more than enough cash flow within the company to make additional funds unnecessary for the time being.

4Refuel's experiences illustrate an important element of a successful growth plan. Raising capital does not always lead directly to the option of significant borrowing from outside sources or an injection of equity. And even when it does, internal discipline in managing finances drives efficiencies in operations that can greatly reduce borrowing costs or the amount of equity a company must yield to outside investors. As a company in the fuel industry, it is rather apt that 4Refuel has been able to run leaner through a tune-up that is delivering much better mileage out of its revenue flow.

As 2011 dawned, 4Refuel had a small presence in the United States, in Seattle, and was considering franchising its business concept in Germany while holding exploratory conversations else-where in Europe as well as in Asia and South America. Gleason says the company had enjoyed "one heck of a growth rate" in Canada and still had abundant domestic opportunities in its business of supplying on-site diesel fuelling to enterprises. "We don't see the growth momentum slowing down in Canada for a long time," he says. "I see so much growth in our own backyard." There was no need to chase opportunities beyond the border when so much new business was close at hand.

The refuelling industry has been growing in Canada for several reasons. Major oil companies have largely abandoned the down-stream business, sometimes keeping naming rights but otherwise selling their interests as they focus their attention and capital on exploration, where the highest returns are promised. That opened up fresh opportunity for a company like 4Refuel, at a time clients were struggling with on-site refuelling. On-site fuel storage was an increasing environmental burden that businesses preferred to elim-inate, and on-site theft of stored fuel was also a headache. 4Refuel was successful in offering two compelling propositions. It was willing to refuel when the customer's fleet wasn't busy, which meant overnight, at 2:00 A.M. if necessary. It also provided a bundled technology solution to management of fuel costs. This was particularly attractive, as in the transportation industry fuel is the largest business cost after labour.

With so much growth still forecast in Canada, 4Refuel sold the Seattle business and put on ice the German franchising initiative and other international opportunities. These had become "a distraction for management," according to Gleason. The company instead focused on growing in Canada through acquisitions of other companies in the refuelling industry or establishing new fleets and people in "greenfield space," cities where 4Refuel wasn't yet operating.

Despite a successful domestic growth initiative, the new credit facility in 2011 remained untapped; the company also was able to dramatically reverse the status of its bank line of credit. When Gleason arrived, the $30 million line was almost maxed out, at $29 million. The line was renegotiated to $40 million to give the company some breathing room, but over the next year, the draw on the line of credit plunged, all while the company was growing.

A chartered accountant, Gleason says the answer to 4Refuel's funding challenges lay within its own financial statements. "The first thing I went to is the balance sheet." The problem—and the solution—for 4Refuel lay in its receivables. On the one hand, receivables are an asset, an implicit promise of impending cash flow. On the other hand, they're a kind of liability, because the longer they take to collect, the longer a company is starved for capital from its own sales. Without the capital to which its sales entitle it, a company has to borrow money in the short term. "Carrying receivables drives borrowing from the bank," Gleason summarizes. In 4Refuel's case, receivables were behind the ever-growing line-of-credit bank facility.

The essential measuring stick of how great a burden receivables can be is the time to collect from the time of invoicing, or day sales outstanding (DSO). When Gleason arrived, DSO at 4Refuel was thirty-four days. It was far too high. "Big oil is operating at ten days on payment, and it's non-negotiable," says Gleason. "Running at thirty-four days on average, we were becoming the bankers for our customers. If a customer is drawing on your capital, it has a negative equity value."

Unless 4Refuel came up with an answer internally, the problem was only going to grow along with the company. The more business the company generated, the more its receivables grew. The problem was exacerbated by the nature of its product. 4Refuel resells diesel fuel on a cost-plus basis. It charges a fixed markup, not a percentage of the wholesale price. A margin of nine or ten cents a litre doesn't change if the price of fuel increases. And as fuel price increased, 4Refuel's need to finance receivables would only increase as well, even though there would be no corresponding increase in profit per litre to cover borrowing costs.

It was one thing to identify the problem. It was another thing to find a solution to it. "We had to educate the client base on the issue. Otherwise we would have to start charging customers like we were bankers." But it wasn't enough just to tell customers they had to get in the habit of paying more quickly. Change had to occur within 4Refuel itself. "There had to be a change of psychology. There were two to three months of education internally," to orient staff to a mindset of driving down day sales. Then 4Refuel had to overhaul its methods and policies.

"We went through with a microscope the delivery-collection process," says Gleason. "We found it was taking five days just to create an invoice." Paper invoices were taking seven days to deliver, and so the switch was made to electronic invoices. To speed up collection, lock boxes for payments were added to client sites to avoid more time lost in the mail. The right to draw payments from client accounts was strongly promoted. New clients were put on a short leash through an "on-boarding process." New clients now sign an agreement on payment terms of ten to fifteen days. "With the very first invoice, we really set expectations. Up front, there's a big effort to change behaviour with new customers. We also increased our invoicing cycle in many instances, going from semi-monthly to weekly invoicing."

To better manage and understand the role of its receivables, 4Refuel developed a software tool to analyze the profitability and balance-sheet impact of individual customers. And in a broader search to define burdens on cash flow, the company audited its own processes with a test of revenue generation. "We asked, 'Are these things part of the growth profile?' There was a lot of internal manual activity that could be automated. We took $1 million out of corporate overheads this way."

Within one year, 4Refuel reduced its DSO from thirty-four days to twenty-five days. "That's a staggering amount," says Gleason. "If we had stayed at thirty-four days and grown the business 26 percent like we did in 2011, our capital requirement would have been in the neighbourhood of $20 million. That's a lot of capital for a company of our size to have freed up. The $29 million in receivables on our line of credit went down to $17 million. Our goal is to get day sales to twenty-two in the next two years."

John Gleason's advice to fellow executives is to take a closer look at their own processes and cash flow before determining how much money they need to borrow. "People get really focused on P&L, and not on their balance sheet. Before you go to the bank to borrow, you need to be asking, 'Is there anything I can do internally? Where is my capital being tied up? What can I do to free up cash?'"

● ● ●

In 2011, JV Driver Group of Leduc, Alberta, secured a multi-million-dollar lending facility with a major Canadian charter bank, which included an operating facility that allows the group of companies to borrow as a consolidated group on a net basis. It was one of the few facilities of its kind that the bank had ever arranged in the construction industry and indicated the degree of confidence the lender had in JV Driver's ability to manage its cash needs prudently.

Starting from nothing, over the past twenty years, JV Driver Group has grown organically and through acquisition to become a diverse conglomerate of construction companies that executes projects in the industrial, civil, commercial/high-rise, and marine industries, particularly in Western Canada. Pursuing a long-term strategy as a vertically integrated contractor that provides a suite of services, including innovative "single site, single source" fabrication, the company has undertaken projects with budgets ranging from $500,000 to $750 million. Its commitment to worker safety has produced an exceptional record: fourteen straight years without a lost-time incident in the field, during more than twenty million worker-hours of construction. In 2010, JV Driver received the Best Safety Performer Award from Alberta Workplace Safety for the fourth consecutive year. In July and August 2011, its safety performance earned it the Golden Nugget Award from its client Imperial Oil. Not surprisingly, "Taking Care of Each Other" is one of the company's core values.

JV Driver says "human capital" is its most precious resource. Historically, projects with superior safety records have often led to higher quality of production and lower overall costs. Executing projects safely thus allows it to live up to another core value: "Build

Great Things." While workplace safety may not seem like the most logical place to approach managing capital and financing, in JV Driver's case it speaks to the company's commitment to detail, to reportage and process, and to managing risk with the goal of eliminating as much of it as possible.

JV Driver divides the task of raising capital and managing finances into four areas: equity growth and intelligent reinvestment, prudent treasury management and cash preservation, strength in stakeholder relationships, and prudent risk management.

"Equity growth is very important to us as a relatively young player in an industry where the customer and competition are sometimes much larger than we are," says chief financial officer Chuck Sanders. "We can't neglect long-term equity growth on the balance sheet." JV Driver considers long-term equity growth a measure of corporate success because of both the cyclical nature of the construction industry and the long-term nature of its project base, especially in the industrial sector. "We guard balance-sheet growth carefully, as this strength is key to managing up and down cycles."

In comparison, it's easier, says Sanders, for a public company to add equity to the balance sheet and deploy it in a "let's have a party" manner. But in a privately held company like JV Driver, "reinvesting equity in the company is the key to growth. That discipline has been an engine for our success. It's important as well to external stakeholders, such as bonding agencies, and banks." Those stakeholders like to see more than top-line (or even bottom-line) performance. Reinvestment that builds equity in JV Driver's industry especially gives reassurance of long-term growth and commitment to building an enterprise that can weather the business cycle's troughs. "Reinvestment is always an engine of growth and the first place you should look to for financing."

Cash preservation and prudent treasury management are a priority in that "access to capital and cash management in a construction setting is absolutely critical." Forecasting cash needs, Sanders feels, is often neglected by businesses in general. The actual forecasting tools and processes may be in place, but a company needs to know realistically where that cash flow is going to come from. Prudent treasury management means knowing you've got enough cash now and also where you're headed where those needs are concerned. "It's a tough thing to do, but once you get into the cadence of accountability, it's a valuable tool in managing cash flow."

One error that Sanders says companies can make is to forecast results in the income statement without knowing where the company is going to be on the balance sheet. This can be particularly the case when, depending on the revenue recognition methods used, accrual accounting creates a divergence between income as recorded with a particular set of accounting rules and actual cash flow and reserves.

Sanders says savvy forecasting requires a clear distinction between leading and lagging indicators. "Leading indicators tell you what's going to happen, and they give you time to correct a trend or to capitalize greater on an opportunity. Without leading indicators, at best you'll see information one month after it happens. You're flying blind only using historic information. You're amplifying your risk." The goal is to manage a company into the future, rather than act based on what has already happened. "It's windshield management versus rear-view mirror management."

Forecasting happens at least monthly at JV Driver, with some crucial leading indicator data in dashboard tools, including forward-looking estimates, compiled weekly. "We've invested in people and systems to provide that level of information. While it isn't perfect yet, we are committed to fine-tuning it, and see it as crucial to our business strategy."

Strength in stakeholder relationships is built with long-term dedication in order to avoid short-term crises. The moment capital is required is not the time to look around wondering what institution can provide it. "One of my jobs is to make sure we know all our potential stakeholders, whether we already have relationships or not." It's important not only to manage relationships a company already has, but to know where such relationships can be forged, if and when they are necessary or advantageous. "The lag time in forming trusting relationships can be years."

JV Driver pays close attention to balance-sheet indebtedness. The amounts are important, but so is the lender behind them. Every debt is an obligation, and an obligation is fundamentally a relationship. "We closely value and manage the relationships that are represented in the liabilities on the balance sheet," says Sanders. "We give them frequent updates. We treat them as a partner. It pays dividends in relationships, and they're there a lot quicker for you when you need them."

Operational lenders, Sanders says, "are largely betting on management." They have their own needs for an effective relationship with management. And if there isn't an ongoing relationship, "they need time to get up to speed" when a company has fresh borrowing needs. JV Driver is always looking for an opportunity to engage their lenders in matters that have nothing to do with a specific borrowing request. "We never miss an opportunity for a plant tour, or to sit down and have lunch and update them on our business," says Sanders.

The final component of sound financial planning at JV Driver is prudent risk management. "Risk elevates in our industry as economies go downward," says Sanders, looking back on the downturn that construction experienced from 2008 to 2010. There's increased competition for fewer contracts, and conditions tighten to the advantage of a project owner, causing a contractor's risk to increase dramatically. "During these periods it takes guts and discipline as a contractor to realistically and prudently measure risk in your marketplace and accept only what makes sense. This may result in lower backlogs as competitors take on unacceptable risks, but will result in higher profits and less exposure to industry cyclicality and loss," says Sanders. The same is true in buoyant markets, he notes, where managing risks such as labour availability, productivity lags, and cost escalation are also crucial to profitability and success for both owner and contractor. "No matter what the economic conditions, this is always achieved through discipline and prudent negotiations where sometimes you have to be brave enough to walk away if the risk of an opportunity is not acceptable."

The elemental goal of prudent risk management of course is to maximize opportunities while minimizing downside risks, and doing so requires not only discipline but also appropriate reporting and forecasting tools. "If you don't have the necessary tools," Sanders warns, "you understate the downside and overstate the upside. Having those tools can save your business."

● ● ●

In mid-2008, as the recession bore down on its clients and the Wheels Group felt the burden of its 2006 acquisition bank loan for the Clipper Group, risk management at the company turned to damage control. The company decided to sell IWheels, a process that concluded in June 2009. The Wheels Group had done its best to stem the bleeding of IWheels through expense reduction, but with revenues spiralling downward more quickly than costs could be cut, the ultimate solution had been to exit this aspect of its business entirely.

"What we had learned through previous business experience is that you cannot cut your costs to success," says Jamieson. "You need to work on what I call the numerator, which is sales, as well as the denominator, which is costs. We worked diligently on that through 2009, and 2010 was a better year as we turned a sharp corner. We continued to make our bank payments and manage the bank and business concerns in a positive direction."

The Wheels Group survived its brush with the recession, exiting the light-asset market tied to automotive/OEM and rapidly recovering by focusing on its core non-asset businesses in 2010, all while faithfully paying down the bank debt incurred by the Clipper Group acquisition. In 2011, it renegotiated a new bank term loan with favourable rates to give it forward stability. The company also resolved to focus on continuing to grow organically, as it had historically, with non-asset customer solutions. But it was also considering growth through new acquisitions that would require more capital than cash flow from organic growth could accommodate. "The question became: How do we step it up?" says Peter Jamieson. "We looked at different ways to capitalize the group: more debt, private equity, or public markets. We wanted to stay in control of our destiny and in leadership positions."

Many companies in the Wheels Group's situation, post-recession, have chosen to grow through mergers and acquisitions, in some cases taking advantage of consolidation in some sectors to increase market share or diversify into new opportunities. Low interest rates have made bank borrowing, whether through term loans or lines of credit, attractive to companies that do not wish to surrender equity. As for the equity side, public markets have given way overwhelmingly to private equity, and we are seeing investment activity by U.S. funds in Canadian companies that would not have been imagined ten or fifteen years ago.

A major player in Canada is OMERS Private Equity, which draws on the capital resources of one of the country's largest pension funds, the Ontario Municipal Employees Retirement System, which manages about $55 billion in net investment assets on behalf of 420,000 members.

"There is still a lot of capital in the market," says Don Morrison, senior managing director and country head, Canada, at OMERS Private Equity. "That's true internationally, as we have offices in Toronto, New York, and London." Banks, too, are active on the lending side. "They are more susceptible to global and local economies, and we've seen ups and downs in their efforts. In 2007–08 we thought we saw the end of banks being aggressive in lending, but it didn't take very long for them to get back in the game, with more aggressive terms."

The big trend in private equity, says Morrison, is the increasing presence of funds like OMERS. "Pension plans have become more active in investing in alternative assets like private equity over the last few years, and this trend has been led by Canadian pension plans. The funds are eliminating the middle man." These plans are entering into direct investments with longer time horizons than a typical private equity fund, which normally expects to make a return over four to seven years and then exit. "Pension funds have the flexibility to be a much longer-term investor," says Morrison.

A significant change that has accompanied direct investment by pension funds is a more proactive role in bringing more tools and resources to investee company management. "Typically, passive equity investors rely on good governance and holding management teams to account. They tend not to engage that actively in the company to help get the job done," says Mike Lank, senior managing director and head of the operations team at OMERS Private Equity. "The other extreme is taking a very hands-on role alongside management, even to the point of acting as an interim resource within senior management. Taking a more active role in working with portfolio management teams is becoming a call to action for many pension funds. Traditional pension funds are exploring this model closely. Some are actively staffing up with the team needed to engage more deeply in their companies. They're asking what they can do across a portfolio of assets to get the benefits of scale and leverage best practices, and what they can do discreetly within an asset to unlock value."

These private-equity funds are proactively plugging gaps in management capability to better ensure the desired return. "Often, many mid-size companies don't have someone dedicated to special projects," Morrison explains. "They're operating lean, and might simply not have the right resources to dedicate to critical initiatives, like the pursuit of an M&A target. This is where we can lend a hand with our expertise." In addition, OMERS Private Equity populates their investee company board of directors with seasoned industry experts. "It can be a lonely as a CEO," Morrison says. "We want to bring in resources, people who have been there, who have been CEOs, who they can talk to. We create an 'office of CEO resource' that helps get the job done."

Lank says OMERS Private Equity is spending an increasing amount of time not just on the thesis for why it likes an asset, but on what OMERS plans to do with it. That means "ensuring that the top two or three key value drivers are well understood and that management is laser focused on them, with the resources it needs to be successful."

● ● ●

The solution the Wheels Group arrived at for funding its continued growth was a plan to move from being a private company to become an ambitious blend of public equity and private placement, successfully executed in a market that was still shy post-recession about companies going public through an IPO. The Wheels Group decided to use a reverse takeover, or RTO. The Wheels Group also had the opportunity to acquire Synergix Logistics, which would provide end-to-end logistics solutions to the electronics and retail markets, which are generally a higher-margin area for 3PLs. It also wanted to put itself in a position to readily execute further growth through acquisitions, drawing up a target list and forming M&A and due diligence teams, crafting a profile of what an attractive acquisition would look like.

"We found an opportunity to acquire an existing company called Greenfield Financial Group, that traded on the TSX Venture Exchange," says Jamieson. The series of transactions are complex, and included a private placement by the combined company and the acquisition of Synergix. When the steps were completed, Greenfield Financial Group had become Wheels Group Inc. on the TSX Venture Exchange in January 2012, and the company had netted approximately $15 million that it could use to pursue growth strategies, which could include an expansion of existing service lines, new services, acquisitions, and working capital for marketing and general operations.

"Moving from private to public status is huge," says Jamieson. Private financials have had to be converted to public standards just as those standards were changing, as Canadian generally accepted accounting principles (GAAP) was being replaced by International Financial Reporting Standards (IFRS). On top of that, the Wheels Group has had to manage the amalgamation of three organizations—Wheels, Clipper, and Synergix—into one operating environment.

Jamieson says the transition to a public company has been much smoother than it could have been because the Wheels Group has effectively been preparing for that day for years. "There's a different regimen of boards, with committees for compensation, audit, and governance, for example. But we had an advisory board through the 2000s, with outside experts helping us improve best practices. And having access to public capital has strengthened our balance sheet."

"If you have the capabilities and the experience, this is a very effective way to continue to grow a company," Jamieson says of the acquisition through a reverse takeover. The company's focus is now on future growth. "The market for transportation in North America is huge, about $1.5 trillion in overall spend. Most people don't understand how big, or how diversified, it is." Half of the market is held by trucking companies, he says, with another 15 percent in rail, and 10 percent in non-asset 3PL companies like Wheels Inc. Within those segments, the competition is highly fragmented. The biggest trucking companies, he notes, hold less than 3 percent of the trucking market. The two largest 3PLs combined account for less than 1 percent of the total transportation market. There are plenty of opportunities for acquisitions at the Wheels Group, whether they are standalone divisions or tuck-unders for existing operations. And because of the reverse takeover, the Wheels Group is positioned to use both cash and its own shares as equity for those acquisitions. It has effectively created a pool of currency with its public stock. "We think we can double size of the company in three years," says Jamieson.

● ● ●

No single strategy in managing capital and funding growth works for all companies, in all circumstances. We have seen how a bank loan to fund growth caused such challenges for the Wheels Group when the recession intruded, yet we have also seen how important a bank credit facility has been to JV Driver in the construction industry. Balance sheet discipline and improving internal processes has been elemental to 4Refuel's cash flow gains, yet the Wheels Group's experience has also shown that a company cannot expect simply to cut costs towards profitability if revenues are declining.

For companies today seeking funds to fuel growth, there are abundant options, even if the IPO market remains challenging. "There's no shortage of investors wanting to place capital—a lot of dry powder that will take years to deploy," says Don Morrison of OMERS Private Equity. All of that pent-up capital at private equity firms and pension funds, combined with the renewed lending enthusiasm of banks, has made for a very competitive capital market. "Privately held companies have a good ability to raise debt financing, because banks are definitely open for business. If the banks are being aggressive, then there are strong valuations for manager/owners. They have a lot of flexibility, a lot of choice."

Manager/owners of privately held companies, Morrison advises, need to be clear in their objectives where private equity is concerned. "Do they want to cash out, or do they want to take something off the table but continue to operate the business?" Companies must be crisp in defining their objectives, and must demonstrate discipline to both lenders and investors in pursuing goals. The required prudence is expressed through risk management, because what are ultimately at risk are the shareholders' equity and the lender's capital.

The dream of perfected risk management, says JV Driver's Chuck Sanders, is first to see the risks, then to mitigate the downside and only capitalize on the upside. "If you can do that," Sanders says, "the sky is the limit, and we all chase that."

# 6

# MERGERS AND ACQUISITIONS: MAKING INSTEAD OF BREAKING BY MATCHING CULTURES

Modern Niagara Group, a mechanical contractor based in Ottawa and active in seven provinces, made its first acquisition in 1992. "We were principally providing mechanical contracting services focused on plumbing and piping, and we were asked by a client if we could provide a total mechanical package," recalls CEO Tony Sottile. An Ottawa-based sheet-metal contractor, Gorlan Mechanical, was available, and Modern Niagara Group decided to acquire it in order to diversify its offerings vertically. Sheet metal work typically represented the group of companies' most significant subcontract cost component, so the acquisition offered immediate financial benefits. At the same time, it would allow Modern Niagara to provide complete mechanical services to clients in the Ottawa area.

The acquisition, says Sottile, went well, although it took a long time to complete the integration, and Modern Niagara Group found ways to speed up that process in subsequent deals. "We learned a lot through it. The biggest lesson is: Numbers are important, but it's all about the culture. If you cannot match the culture, the acquisition will be a failure. It's that simple. Culture is not a spreadsheet document. You have to get into the weeds and learn what it is."

•   •   •

Not all growth can be, or should be, organic, which is to say driven by incremental increases in sales by existing operations. Many companies, at some point in their history, have the opportunity to merge with or acquire another enterprise.

We've witnessed a particular focus recently on merger-and-acquisition activity among Canada's Best Managed Companies winners. This has involved not only business acquisitions, but related initiatives like strategic alliances and joint ventures where skills, scale, and geographic presence can be of mutual benefit, either long-term or in single projects. Private equity has played a leading role in funding M&A activity, and Canadian companies have proven to be especially attractive targets, particularly as industries have emerged from the recent recession. There have been prime opportunities to increase market share with "tuck under" or "bolt on" acquisitions that add capacity or capability to an existing division. Such acquisitions can improve business diversification by integrating new products and services that are aligned to the current customer base. Companies also have been pursuing "step out" acquisitions that allow them to expand into entirely new areas of business, reaching new markets and customers.

The companies discussed in this chapter have long histories of acquisition. The growth they have pursued has been both horizontal and vertical. Some acquisitions have arisen from long working relationships that included formal joint-venture partnerships on particular projects, with both companies recognizing that they have more to gain through a merger of capital and an integrated operation than an ongoing collaboration. Growth through acquisition is critical to a business gaining scale and ensuring its competitiveness.

In technology-reliant businesses, an acquisition can deliver valuable intellectual property far less expensively (and with far greater marketplace certainty) than attempts to develop it from scratch in-house. Combining with a competitor can deliver greater scale to operations, improving revenues and market share while reducing costs through rationalization. There are myriad reasons for proceeding. Knowing when *not* to proceed can be one of the harder lessons to learn. Sometimes the deal not done proves to be the best way forward.

The companies we meet here have been able to post high batting averages where successful acquisitions are concerned because they have not allowed the temptation of deals to distract them from their strategic objectives. While opportunistic acquisitions often are the norm, corporate strategy must always prevail when deciding to act on opportunity. Moreover, success is based on ensuring a fundamentally sound fit. And that fit is not just products or services—as the Modern Niagara Group's Tony Sottile stresses, it's culture.

● ● ●

The Modern Niagara Group's twelve companies focus on mechanical contracting and engineering for new construction in the industrial, commercial, and institutional (ICI) sectors, as well as heating, ventilation, and air-conditioning (HVAC) services.

"We build things, we're low tech, and we like being low tech," says CEO Tony Sottile, who has been with the Modern Niagara Group for twenty-one years and has served as CEO for the past seven. Its specialties are public–private partnerships (P3) and design-build. While the company still takes on many tendered projects, "We've moved up the food chain."

Modern Niagara Group is fifty-four years old and was first named one of Canada's Best Managed Companies in 1996. There have been significant changes over the last seven years under Sottile's leadership. Those changes have been due substantially to an acquisition-based growth strategy. The Modern Niagara Group's aim is to control construction costs through vertical diversification, avoiding reliance on subcontractors to estimate, bid, and perform major projects. Indeed, without the diversification achieved through acquisitions, the Modern Niagara Group would not have reached the present stage where it is capable of bidding on major P3 projects. These acquisitions have given Modern Niagara Group crucial cost control. Cost certainty allows it to bid more competitively and with confidence. It does not have to fear budget surprises from subcontractors, and by owning an enterprise it has the necessary visibility to contain costs and operate efficiently in the aspects of projects that account for a large proportion of a bid's value.

One of its most important acquisitions, Toronto's DMC Mechanical, was completed in November 2009. DMC was (and remains) a prime sheet-metal contractor operating in the same geographic area as the group's business, Modern Niagara Toronto. DMC had worked with Modern Niagara Toronto for many years, partnering on design-build projects, and the companies decided to make that relationship formal. DMC would operate as a separate company within the group and have a similar relationship with Modern Niagara Toronto that the 1992 acquisition Gorlan Mechanical has with Modern Niagara Ottawa. DMC would continue managing its own clientele while supporting Modern Niagara Toronto on combined project tenders. DMC's downtown Toronto division and special projects group also neatly mirrored the structure of Modern Niagara Toronto.

The Modern Niagara Group had made a shrewd strategic acquisition: It could now control all of the significant mechanical construction costs in the bidding process in the Toronto market as well as the P3 markets. In keeping with the strategy, in 2007 it acquired a Halifax full-service mechanical contractor with an in-house sheet-metal operation, which was rebranded as Atlantica Mechanical. Along with the acquisition of DMC, the Modern Niagara Group had three sheet-metal manufacturing facilities responsible for producing four to five million pounds of ductwork per year. In 2011, the Modern Niagara Group also purchased a second sheet-metal shop in Toronto in order to complete its Humber River Hospital project.

The Modern Niagara Group chose M&A as its active strategy growth through diversifying acquisitions. Once it did so, says Sottile, "our goal was to be extremely flexible, to be able to react to opportunities. One thing is to have the cash in the bank. The other is to have the senior management capacity to address them."

To be successful in pursuing M&A as a growth strategy, a company needs to be nimble, Sottile advises. "These things happen quite quickly. If someone knocks on our door, they're already in a frame of mind to get something done. It puts huge pressure on due diligence. Looking back, it was like the 'wild west' in how much due diligence we were able to do in such a short period of time."

The Modern Niagara Group chooses its acquisition opportunities by focusing on the target's core competencies. "We ask, 'What is a company really good at?'" says Sottile. "We then take away from companies the things they don't like to do. In construction, companies typically don't like paperwork and the back-end office stuff. We like to do those things and are quite good at them, and this is the true synergy. By letting the company focus on building and the projects on hand, we find we get our true payback."

The Modern Niagara Group has invested significantly in that "back end," and in 2011 embarked on a SharePoint Business Intelligence initiative to test and prove the effectiveness of the framework within the group of companies. The results clearly indicated that SharePoint could be the cornerstone of its management information system at all levels of the business. "What has made us better at M&A, and has given us the confidence to do it, is that we've developed a strong back end, in functions like IT, relative to our industry. We've invested heavily in this area and believe this will bring our management systems and our ability to share information to a new level," Sottile explains.

Next to the need to be satisfied that there is a good culture match, Sottile says, the most important lesson has been that an acquisition needs an executive assigned to it full-time to ensure it works. "If we can't assign a senior partner or a vice-president to oversee the integration, we're just not going to do it. The numbers can line up, but you need to have someone on top of it 24/7."

Sottile says the Modern Niagara Group learned that lesson the hard way, with a rare failure. "A couple of years ago we had a chance to acquire a company, which was virtually free. We went ahead, but we didn't check the culture and did not have someone on it 24/7, and it was a disaster. This reinforced what we already knew and will never happen again." Adds Sottile, "Opportunities are coming to us without looking for them. But we still are making sure the culture works and that we have senior people in place."

●  ●  ●

The importance, stressed by the Modern Niagara Group's Tony Sottile, of ensuring a good culture match is shared by other companies with deep experience in acquisitions. John Leder, president and COO of Edmonton's Supreme Group, Canada's largest privately owned steel construction company, considers corporate culture an important factor in making an acquisition succeed. "The employees of an acquisition have to be integrated into your culture, but they have to feel they have a place in it," he says. "We try to keep management in place. I don't think we've ever parachuted people in. It's not the building and the equipment you want. It's the people. When you've got people that have worked twenty, thirty years, you've got depth, and you can then figure out how to use that depth."

The Supreme Group has not relied exclusively on acquisitions to increase its competitive stance. A case in point is its participation in the construction of The Bow, which at fifty-eight stories truly dominates the Calgary skyline, as much through its unique curved cross-section and construction as through its scale. As the new headquarters of Encana, The Bow has introduced about two million square feet of AAA-rated commercial estate to the heart of Calgary's financial district. It is also the first building in North America to employ an external diagrid system of triangles—each of them six stories tall—that serves as a perimeter frame for the shimmering glass skin. Supreme Group Fabrication executed fabricating, detailing, and erection for the design in a joint venture with Walters Inc. of Ontario. "Topped" in 2011, The Bow allowed Supreme Group to share in the 2011 Engineering Award from the Canadian Institute of Steel Construction (CISC) Alberta.

The Bow is not the only project that the Supreme Group has undertaken through joint ventures, which it has found increasingly useful in addressing project-by-project issues such as enhancing its own capacity (as in the case of The Bow) and providing access to local labour markets. Otherwise, the Supreme Group operates mainly through six operating companies: Supreme Steel of

Edmonton (which has multiple plants); Midwest Constructors of Edmonton; Canron Western Constructors (Canada) of Delta, BC; Canron Western Constructors (US) of Portland, Oregon; Quality Fabrication & Supply of Edmonton; and Hopkin Steelworks of Welland, Ontario.

The Supreme Group began in 1972, when John Leder left his job as a welder with a mid-sized Edmonton company to buy a truck and start servicing field jobs himself. Three years later, Leder moved his fledgling company into the Edmonton facility known as Plant 1, where he started to do fabrication work in addition to installations in the field. Supreme Steel evolved into the Supreme Group as Leder, who remains the majority shareholder, expanded his operation in Western Canada. Growth—and survival— depended on regional diversification to avoid the volatility of the resource-driven Alberta construction market. Determined reinvestment helped Supreme along, and much of its growth came through acquisitions.

Companies electing to use mergers and acquisitions for growth arrive at their deals through different methods and along diverse avenues. "We don't really target outfits," says the Supreme Group's John Leder. "All acquisitions have come to us, and never through a broker. The principals or someone in management have approached us." And a good percentage, says Leder, have been someone saying, "John, we're in trouble. Help us out."

Steel fabrication is a tough, competitive business in North America, and domestic enterprises have faced strong competition from overseas in bids for major projects. It's been this way for many years, and cries for help are how Leder and the Supreme Group got into making major acquisitions.

The first significant one was in 1989—a steel-fabricating company in Saskatoon. "A friend called and said, 'John, we've got trouble.' I found out he'd been dealing with about five different banks. We ended up buying pieces of the company from different banks." It became the Saskatchewan branch of Supreme Steel.

In 1994, a bridge company in Edmonton became available. "It was an ugly duckling on a public company's books. It wanted to give the company to management for book value. We bought it for book." In 2000, an owner looking to retire approached Leder to take over his business. It became Supreme's quality fabricating company. And in June 2003, Leder was presented with the opportunity to acquire Canron Western. He visited the operation in September and had a deal in October.

In 2011, Supreme acquired an interest in a Vancouver Island metal-fabrication company and made a strategic investment in iSPAN, an Ontario company developing new technology for long-span floor joists. And on October 30, 2011, Supreme signed a letter of intent to acquire Empire Iron Works, a metal fabricator in Winnipeg that had been performing work for Supreme for some time, along with Hopkin Steelworks in Welland, Ontario—both from Empire Industries of Winnipeg. The deal was concluded in January 2012, and Empire Iron Works became Supreme Steel's Winnipeg division.

Looking back on the many acquisition opportunities that have come along, Leder reflects: "Some of these companies were well managed, and we were in the right time and place. Some just lacked the capital and couldn't function." Without capital, they were incapable of bidding on projects at a scale necessary to their survival. Competition and difficulties in access to capital have created a recipe for consolidation, and the Supreme Group has been able to strengthen itself as the consolidator.

Perhaps because so many of the company's acquisitions have arisen from personal relationships, Leder has found that it's best if he serves as the point person on Supreme's acquisitions. "I've tried to delegate," he says, "but it doesn't work." Dealing with the acquisitions first-hand is especially important because he views trust as the essential ingredient.

"I don't get too fussy over little details," says Leder. Supreme has an in-house counsel, but on a recent acquisition he hired outside representation in the city where the deal was being done. "They fussed over details we didn't need to. If you approach the acquisition from a point of view of trust and fairness, it should go quickly."

● ● ●

Another company to have based its growth fundamentally on acquisitions is Groupe Deschênes of Montreal. In 1940, François Miville-Deschênes bought Langelier & Fils, which was founded in 1936. It became Deschênes & Fils Ltée, a plumbing and heating wholesaler on Notre-Dame East in Montreal. Acquisitions however did not begin in earnest until 1980, when Les Enterprises Mirca, the family business created in 1976 by François Miville-Deschênes's grandson, Jacques, acquired L.N. & J.E. Noiseux Limitée, a century-old plumbing and heating wholesaler in Montreal. In all, Groupe Deschênes (created in 1988) would make some two-dozen acquisitions—and counting—over the coming years.

Groupe Deschênes historically has focused on two areas of construction supplies: plumbing and heating. Its full product line now includes electrical and industrial supplies; fire protection products; ventilation, air conditioning, and refrigeration (HVAC/R); and waterworks and sewer systems. Its expansion efforts have been both "tuck under" and "bolt on," aimed at diversifying geographically and in sales channels. Acquisitions have extended its presence as far west as Alberta and into both contractor sales and some consumer retailing. It is now one of the leading plumbing and heating product wholesalers in Canada, with eight operational centres, more than ninety outlets, and some thirteen hundred employees, generating sales in excess of $500 million.

From Groupe Deschênes's perspective, "The construction industry is not really growing," explains Martin Deschênes, grandson of François Miville-Deschênes. He became Groupe Deschênes's president and chief operating officer in 2000 and assumed the role of CEO in 2004 from his father Jacques, who has continued to serve on the board. "It's a mature market. The only way to grow is to take market share from competitors, and the only way for a company to grow within is to compete heavily or to acquire other businesses."

Groupe Deschênes arrived in the Ontario market with the acquisition of Ottawa's Boone Plumbing and Heating Supply in 1987. Above and beyond a series of acquisitions in Quebec, in 1990 it acquired Rocamora Bros. Canada, a Toronto-based plumbing and heating distributor/wholesaler; the following year, it acquired Triangle Plumbing and Heating Supply, which had six branches in northern and eastern Toronto. In 1996, it secured a significant interest in Almacorp Inc., a major distributor of air-conditioning and refrigeration parts and equipment, which included nine branches operating under the name Airco and QuéMar in Ottawa, Quebec City, and Montreal. The company arrived in Edmonton in 1997 by becoming a partner in a plumbing and heating distributor, JBW Pipe & Supply. In 2005, it absorbed Bardon Supplies Ltd., a plumbing and HVAC distributor/wholesaler with twelve outlets and four showrooms in Ontario. A further major acquisition was made in 2010, when Groupe Deschênes completed its purchase of Mueller Flow Control, an eighteen-outlet operation based in Stoney Creek, Ontario, which was renamed Flocor. And in 2011, the group acquired two new retail outlets, in Mascouche, Quebec, and Guelph, Ontario.

Groupe Deschênes has identified acquisitions as a key part of its four strategic vectors, aiming to increase sales and profits by acquisitions as well as by organic growth. "We have done about twenty-five acquisitions in our history," Martin Deschênes affirms. "But we cannot put aside the fact that our business has also grown significantly organically. In 2010, our sales above and beyond Flocor increased over 20 percent."

Without organic growth, acquisitions would simply mask a steady decline in revenues and market share, patching holes in an increasingly larger, more top-heavy, and more leaky ship. And without paying attention to its other strategic vectors, Groupe Deschênes would never be able to capitalize on the opportunities those acquisitions presented. Poorly considered and executed acquisitions would jeopardize the entire business model, confounding efforts to follow the other vectors. These vectors call upon Groupe Deschênes to improve its operational and business processes, to understand and meet the needs of its clients, and to ensure the development of its human capital, by assuring its employees' future, personal growth, and financial health. The group's longstanding acquisition rigour and operational excellence has been well recognized. Groupe Deschênes was first recognized as one of Canada's Best Managed Companies in 1994.

"We have to take care of our business," Deschênes says. "We have to work on our detailed processes and consult with customers to see what we can do better."

Before Groupe Deschênes makes an acquisition, "we have to be convinced there is a fit," says Deschênes. "There are companies we have not bought because they didn't fit philosophically. We also try to make sure we keep the entrepreneurial spirit of each company."

The group is organized into eight companies (not including its interest in the Edmonton partnership). Each company retains its own management group. "It makes us closer to the customer than having me in the corner office," says Deschênes. Every business, every outlet, has unique characteristics that cannot be micro-managed from a central corporate office. "One of our companies in Ottawa has a sandwich shop in it," Deschênes offers as an example. "A large part of its business is driven through counter sales. But sales at some of our other places are driven through deliveries."

Groupe Deschênes has been careful to delineate the areas in which its operating companies require independence and the "non-negotiable" areas in which the group must assert system-wide standards and controls. The Supreme Group follows much the same acquisition regimen. Aspects of operations like quality assurance and control and drafting systems might vary slightly, but Supreme ensures that acquisitions are fully integrated in back-office systems like accounting and IT.

At Groupe Deschênes, all financial processes and reportage are handled by the group's system, as a single IT system is managed corporately. The group also acts quickly to integrate an acquisition. Flocor, for example, was acquired in January 2010, and by April the following year, its eighteen-outlet operation had been brought into the corporate ERP management and information systems. Standards in human resources are also enforced group-wide.

"When we make an acquisition, HR people are in right away," says Deschênes. While front-line HR duties like hirings still occur at the individual company level, HR policies remain aligned with the group's strategy. "The vice-president of human resources ensures that our ways of doing things are respected throughout the group." Purchasing is similarly managed. Day-to-day purchasing remains at the individual company level, but strategic issues are the domain of the group's vice-president of procurement.

Groupe Deschênes has long invested heavily in technology to create the corporate backbone that supports group-wide processes while also giving front-line employees the tools to maximize customer service. Like the Modern Niagara Group, this has given the company capabilities that may be lacking elsewhere in its own industry and has provided much more certainty in integrating an acquisition. Its telephone ordering system can redirect calls to other locations to fill orders when the outlet a customer has called is busy, for example. It is also developing a Web-based sales presence and formed ten discussion groups composed of staff as well as customers to determine the specifications for a system it expects to introduce in 2013.

•　•　•

Companies who succeed in growing through acquisitions understand the human factor. Like the Modern Niagara Group, they focus foremost on compatible corporate cultures. Like the Supreme Group, they view the employees and management of an acquisition as the real acquisition, not the land and machinery. Like Groupe Deschênes, they understand that acquired enterprises need to be able to act locally within the system framework of the parent organization. It prioritizes customer service and satisfaction and support of front-line staff while ensuring uniformity of key systems and processes like finance, information technology, and human resources.

"I don't think there's a magic recipe in managing companies," says Martin Deschênes of Group Deschênes. "We make sure our people are well entrenched in their business." He espouses a reverse-pyramid approach to management in which the widest part, at the top, is the front-line employee. "Those employees who deal with customers on a daily basis should get the most attention from the organization."

"We've had a very good retention rate in the management of companies we've bought," Tony Sottile of the Modern Niagara Group notes, underscoring the successes in matching cultures. "Sometimes we haven't bought 100 percent of a company. We have maintained the management team and left them with some equity. Our group is a decentralized management model, so we're comfortable with that. We've never driven our company at the group level of revenues. We're driven from the grassroots."

Some of the Supreme Group's acquisitions have followed a similar model of leaving some equity with the target company's owners. It's a model Supreme has striven to refine. "Smaller companies often think they're worth more," says John Leder, "so you say, 'Prove it to me.' We'll buy 40 to 50 percent, or 51 percent. We'll let the existing ownership keep the rest, but we have the option to buy the rest in two to four years. We don't risk as much capital, and owners can earn a better deal by growing the company over the next few years. They can get a lot more for their second half than they did for their first half. And they can use the money to buy Supreme Group units under the employee ownership plan."

To some degree, companies that undertake acquisitions expect to be changed by them, as that is the nature of growth. The challenge remains how to ensure best practices are quickly introduced in the acquisition, without compromising the essential marketplace strengths that attracted the purchaser in the first place. New technologies and information systems can be introduced. An organization's culture, on the other hand, is more difficult to change for the better and unfortunately easier to change for the worse.

In making a corporate match, the values of organizations matter far more than the state of their receivables or the nature of their accounting software. As the Modern Niagara Group's Tony Sottile stresses, if under the pressure to complete an acquisition "you're going to mess up, do it on the nitty-gritty of due diligence. Never mess up on the culture side."

# 7

# INNOVATION: HOW TRENDSETTING COMPANIES EMBRACE A CULTURE OF CHANGE

Ask most people to name a recent innovation in consumer products and they'll likely mention touch-screen smartphones, 3D televisions, or cars that parallel-park themselves. They're highly unlikely to cast their minds back to the last time they visited a supermarket dairy case, but if they did, they'd realize that there were egg products they simply would not have seen in the mid-1990s. There are free-run, Omega 3, and reduced-cholesterol eggs, and liquid egg products in cartons like white-only and French toast mix, to name but a few novelties of the past dozen years. Packaging too has changed—to become more recyclable and environmentally friendly. The egg industry, which had remained predictable in its offerings for decades, has been experiencing a flurry of product innovation, much of it driven by one Canadian company, Burnbrae Farms.

"Before 1996, none of our innovative products existed," says Margaret Hudson, who was a vice-president of sales and marketing at Burnbrae Farms before becoming company president. "Over 90 percent of production in the early 1990s was grade 'A' large. Free-run didn't exist, or organic."

Burnbrae's product diversification (and outright creation of new product categories) over the past dozen years exemplifies a key trend in innovation we've seen among Canada's Best Managed Companies. Innovations aren't giving rise to mass production/low-cost offerings. Instead they tend to be found in adding value, in focusing on higher-margin products and services in order to increase both revenue and profits.

When we speak of "innovation" in business, we invariably think of technology, of hardware and software, of patents and new-product breakthroughs. Those kinds of innovation are important, and in this chapter we do consider companies that have excelled through the introduction of innovative products. But often, as we'll see, bringing new ideas to market can require as much innovation as the innovations themselves.

To be sure, Canada's Best Managed Companies are innovative in all aspects of their business, whether it's managing capital, attracting and retaining talent, or managing brands. Innovation is ultimately about differentiation, and that is as true of the workplace environment offered to prospective employees and the fiscal savvy demonstrated to lenders and investors as it is of the product or service brought to market. If you look only to this chapter for insights into innovation, you will miss the essentially innovative nature of the best practices highlighted in the rest of this book. And as we explain in other chapters, innovation is crucial to improving Canada's labour productivity and the global competitiveness of its enterprises.

In this chapter, we aim to showcase innovation within a narrower band: the development of products, processes, or services that differentiate a company in the marketplace. Such innovation avoids the commoditization of goods and services, which reduces offerings to price points with razor-thin profit margins. Where commoditized product fights for market share, innovative product can create new markets, or become category leaders, with higher margins. Innovation also requires an organization to embrace a culture of continuous improvement. The companies we'll look at in this chapter show that *how* they bring innovations to the market-place can be as important as *what* they bring. Innovation is not limited to a different restaurant menu item, or a water-treatment technology, or a new form of broadcasting, or a novel product for the supermarket dairy case. Innovative companies are committed to being advanced in all aspects of the enterprise, and their leader-ship drives a "change" agenda. We see this throughout the ranks of Canada's Best Managed Companies winners. It's about constantly striving to be better at what you do and how you do it.

● ● ●

Burnbrae Farms Ltd. is a remarkable story of a family business that began more than a century ago with a single 100-acre farm outside the village of Lyn, near Brockville in eastern Ontario. Joseph Hudson arrived from Stranraer in western Scotland to begin farming in the late 1800s. In 1893, he bought the farm near Lyn and called it Burnbrae, "burn" being a Scottish word for stream and "brae" a hillside, both of which were appropriate to this modest plot of land. Today, the Hudson family presides over the largest inte-grated egg supplier in Canada, selling over 35 percent of the shell eggs and over 80 percent of retail liquid egg products. Through egg production, grading stations, and manufacturing facilities, Burnbrae has a presence in British Columbia, Alberta, Manitoba, Ontario, and Quebec. More than 300 egg producers reach the market through Burnbrae's grading stations. While most of its sales are to the consumer market through major retailers, Burnbrae also enjoys significant sales to food service operations (including restaurant chains) and large bakeries that require eggs as ingredients.

Burnbrae's evolution was relatively prolonged. It was a dairy operation until the family took the first step into egg production in 1943, when Joseph Hudson's grandson, Joe (who is Burnbrae's CEO), raised fifty chicks to egg-laying hens as a high-school project. By 1948, three thousand chickens were producing eggs alongside the family's dairy and cash-crop efforts. The family farm's future was firmly allied with egg production in 1956 when it began grading eggs and acquired its first grocery account, Steinberg's in Montreal.

Burnbrae evolved with and adapted to the egg-quota systems that began to appear provincially in the 1960s and were organized under a national supply management regimen in 1972. (Today, eggs are one of five agricultural products that are supply-managed in Canada; the others are milk, turkeys, chicken, and broiler hatching eggs.) Managing their egg supply within a quota system is one of Burnbrae's core competencies, says Joe's daughter Margaret Hudson, president of Burnbrae Farms Ltd. "Our egg grading stations work with different producers to market their eggs. We're always making sure we have the right mix of eggs for our own products. Once you have production for the different varieties of eggs, you've got to sell them all."

Burnbrae expanded elsewhere in Ontario and into other provinces by establishing new operations and acquiring existing ones, both egg-producing farms and grading stations that gather eggs from other producers. But the enterprise endured years of declining sales in the egg industry overall, as consumers were frightened away by a misunderstood dietary bogeyman called cholesterol. In 1996, Canadian per capita consumption of eggs increased for the first time since 1979, as revised health advice and better understanding of cholesterol began to swing consumers back to eggs. It was right when Burnbrae itself embarked on an unbroken streak of innovation—not only in products but in marketing and business practices.

The Canadian egg industry was on the cusp of tremendous change in product offerings, and Burnbrae would be at the forefront. Burnbrae already had entered the "further processing" market in 1973, establishing a plant in Lyn to break, pasteurize, and package eggs for the bakery, hotel, restaurant, and industrial trade. After years of cooperating with research at the University of Guelph and working with Health Canada on labelling, Burnbrae introduced Naturegg Omega 3, eggs rich in the beneficial fatty acid, in 1996. It was a ribbon winner in the 1997 Canadian Grand Prix New Product Awards. Overseen initially by the Canadian Council of Grocery Distributors and now by the Retail Council of Canada, the Grand Prix awards recognize innovations in food and non-food products on grocery-store shelves. The Naturegg Omega 3 win was soon followed by recognition of the liquid product Simply Egg Whites, nominated in 1998, and Naturegg Break Free, a whole egg liquid replacement that was a winner in two categories in 1999, as best new dairy-category product and All-Canadian product of the year. Naturegg Omega Pro (now Break-Free Omega 3) was a winner in 2000.

Today, Burnbrae produces eggs in three categories: shell, liquid, and cooked. Shell eggs are produced under both the Burnbrae Farms and Naturegg brands, and include Omega 3, free-run, and organic varieties. The liquid product line includes cholesterol-free Simply Egg Whites, and Egg Creations, as well as Break Free, with 80 percent less fat and cholesterol than regular eggs. In 2004, Burnbrae began building a plant in the Brockville area so it could enter the cooked egg market with products like hard-boiled eggs, patties, and omelettes. In 2008, Naturegg Omega 3 hard-boiled eggs won four Grand Prix awards, including All-Canadian New Product of the Year, bringing Burnbrae's wins to date to thirteen—a remarkable run for a company that had only begun marketing its product innovations in 1996. In 2011, two more new products were unveiled in its liquid line: French Toast Mix and Free Run Simply Egg Whites. While developing innovative products for grocery store shelves, Burnbrae was also expanding as a supplier to quick-service restaurants, and serves many chains with shell, processed, and cooked products.

The company's excellence has been recognized well beyond Canada's borders. At the 2011 International Egg Commission (IEC) conference in Washington, DC, Burnbrae was honoured as the egg product company of the year. "Judges declared Burnbrae Farms as the winner in this category," announced the IEC, "in recognition of its excellent product assortment and high-quality product offering. Judges were also very impressed with the company's performance and investment in new technology, innovation, and sustainability programs."

While new consumer products have attracted the most attention for Burnbrae, Margaret Hudson views its innovation track record with much greater breadth and depth. Marketing is an important case in point. "We're not big-budget marketers," she notes. Burnbrae has invested occasionally in a certain amount of television advertising—for example, with the Brand Power promotion for its new line of Egg Creations liquid products in 2007. But it is not a relentless presence in consumer advertising. "We've created new products, but the real success has been in how we manage the shelf presence."

Hudson says that Burnbrae has excelled in "shelf space management" in grocery-store retailing. Burnbrae's category-management skills and strategies within the store environment have benefited both itself and retailers. Signage at the retail level has also been critical to driving sales. Displaying the right products in the right locations within the dairy category has allowed greater penetration of its premium specialty items.

As for promotion, Burnbrae has worked assiduously beyond media purchases and retail signage to promote its products—and eggs in general—as a healthy dietary choice. "We've marketed outside retail stores to health professionals, especially to dieticians." Its corporate website delivers considerable information to consumers about nutrition, as well as resources for nutrition professionals. Having its shell eggs and Naturegg liquid products recognized by the Heart and Stroke Foundation's Health Check program has also paid dividends. Under Health Check, companies and restaurants voluntarily submit products or menu items, which are evaluated by the Foundation's registered dietitians for inclusion, in its nutrition guide.

"An egg is a vessel to grow life," Hudson sums up. "Cholesterol is such an essential nutrient for your life that your body will make it if you don't eat enough of it. The unique thing about eggs is you can eat them every day. And almost everybody eats eggs. They can get extra nutrients without struggling to make changes in their habits."

Margaret Hudson stresses, "Innovation goes beyond products. It's how you approach business. We have a long way to go on corporate responsibility, but we're on the way."

Burnbrae has taken a proactive role on animal welfare. "It's important for us to engage consumers," Hudson says. Back in 2003, Burnbrae was able to secure status as a shell-egg supplier to McDonald's because it could satisfy the company's animal-welfare audit nationally. It continues to work through the Egg Farmers of Ontario, for example, with the Ontario Farm Animal Council (OFAC), which in January 2012 joined with Agricultural Groups

Concerned about Resources and the Environment (AGCare) to form Farm & Food Care Ontario. The united group aims to provide public education about farm practices, including animal welfare. Burnbrae also participates in Canada's Virtual Farm Tours, a website through which consumers can visit working farms. Featured are free-run, free-range, and conventional egg-laying operations. "We're encouraging people to come and see what we do, and we're proud of it."

Burnbrae is also determined to be on the leading edge of carbon footprint reduction, with a goal to one day become carbon-neutral in its operations. "We're at least getting processes in place," Hudson says.

• • •

Innovation in "green" initiatives has become a hallmark of Canada's Best Managed Companies, as we see in Chapter 9, "Sustainability: Doing the Right Things for Customers and Community," and in the case of Cactus Club Cafe, which is the first Canadian restaurant group admitted to the Green Table Network (GTN). Cactus Club in fact was a founding member of GTN in 2007, which is dedicated to reducing the environmental impact of the restaurant industry as well as its suppliers. From ten original members, GTN grew to about one hundred members in British Columbia and in April 2012 was relaunched as a national Web-based initiative. Membership requires an audited commitment to meeting the GTN's core initiatives of solid waste reduction, energy and water conservation, pollution prevention, and sustainable purchasing.

Cactus Club also demonstrates that, while research and development certainly contributes to innovation, the role of R&D varies with industries. In the restaurant business, innovation can involve test kitchens and market research, but the success of Cactus Club as an innovator is substantially due to intuitive creativity. The two defining qualities of the restaurant group's reputation for innovation may well be (1) defy categories and (2) offer customers what they want before they even know they want it.

Founded in 1988 by CEO Richard Jaffray, Cactus Club Cafe restaurants are neither clubs nor cafés, and they challenge the expectations of what a restaurant chain is supposed to be and how it should operate. The restaurant designs are not one-box-fits-all-locales, the menu defies the industry's penchant for strict categorization, the enlistment of celebrity-status food and beverage specialists is unheard of, and its commitment to environmentally responsible menu items is far ahead of the industry curve, particularly for a chain operation.

The restaurant industry is customarily divided into three broad categories: fine dining, casual dining, and quick-service (a.k.a. "fast food"). The categories are certainly fluid, but it is difficult to think of another restaurant chain that is so elusive in its character. Routinely placed in the casual category, Cactus Club has become renowned for its high-low concept. As one food blogger has marvelled, only at Cactus Club can you expect the option of ordering chicken wings or citrus-spiked tuna tataki.

"We definitely push the envelope on the sector," says Jaffray, who was inducted in BC's Restaurant Hall of Fame in 2010. "Cactus Club has been pushing upward into fine dining but keeping within casual as well." With one restaurant experience behind him, Jaffray began planning Cactus Club in 1987 and opened the first one in 1988. "It started with the concept of a quality coffee shop/diner, casual but at a high level." Some of his inspiration was provided by BC's venerable White Spot chain. Since then, Cactus Club has grown to twenty-two outlets in Western Canada while steadily evolving and challenging the boundaries of its category. In 2007, Cactus Club made its first of five consecutive appearances among Canada's Best Managed Companies; in 2008, it earned the first of four consecutive accolades as the best casual restaurant chain by *Vancouver* magazine. It was even recently named the Best Restroom in Canada (for its Byrne Road location in Vancouver) by washroom supply company Cintas Corp.

"We have unique demographics in how broad a range we appeal to," says Jaffray. "We get a very big capture. We can make a lot of people comfortable in 'pockets' in different parts of the restaurant." Different "day parts" also draw different clientele. Seniors might dominate the lunch hour in a particular location, while a younger crowd might be on hand in the evenings for cocktails. "In our downtown Vancouver location, we really appeal to the business community. In Yaletown, we attract more of a young, urban professional customer. We try to create a connection between different Cactus Clubs, so we have designs that suit neighbourhoods and are more sophisticated than a cookie-cutter approach."

Jaffray says Cactus Club strives to abide by the Japanese concept of *kaisan*, of constant, continuous improvement, a concept with more currency in manufacturing than hospitality. "It's been very organic, with a few bigger leaps forward." Two of the most significant leaps came when the chain added two marquee-quality names. Cactus Club caused a genuine media stir in 2008 when it secured chef Rob Feenie as its "food concept architect," overseeing the menu for the entire chain. In 2005, Feenie became the first Canadian to win the Iron Chef America competition, and he now enjoys a significant public profile. He is a regular on *Urban Rush*, a local Vancouver talk show, and contributes monthly to the *Globe and Mail* and CTV's *Marilyn Denis Show*. Renowned sommelier Sebastien Le Goff joined the operations management team as service director in 2011 and was instrumental in opening a new location at English Bay in March 2012.

"We hired Rob because we loved his food," says Jaffray. "But it created more of a media stir than we ever thought it would." The addition of Le Goff and Feenie has helped Cactus Club press the limits of the casual dining envelope even harder. "We're taking their expertise and quality from high-level dining and putting it in an environment with more general appeal."

Social responsibility has become a significant differentiator. As we discuss in Chapter 9, "Sustainability: Doing the Right Things for Customers and Community," Cactus Club has overcome supply-chain obstacles to source locally grown farm fare and has aided one of its suppliers, a freshwater steelhead salmon farm, in becoming endorsed by the Vancouver Aquarium's Ocean Wise sustainable seafood program.

Cactus Club upholds the reputation of innovative companies for a restless quest to drive change. "Some people say, 'If it isn't broke, don't fix it,'" says Jaffray. "We say, 'We're going to fix it before it's broke.' If things aren't changing, it drives our people crazy. Our organization is resistant to things standing still. We're serving items many competitors have tried in the casual/fine-dining space but haven't been able to achieve as standard items. If you wait to innovate until to you need to, it's way too late."

Restaurants in general constantly struggle with two opposing forces among clientele: a desire for the predictable and the favourite, and a yearning for novelty. Consumer tastes change. If those tastes move more quickly than a restaurant's offerings do, a business will confront expensive efforts to recapture lost clientele with a revital-ization program that may be beyond the capabilities of a staid corporate culture to execute.

"There are customers who say they want things that are new,

but they still order the old items," says Jaffray. Having Rob Feenie's name on the menu has helped "get customers out of their comfort zone," Jaffray notes. "I've had friends tell me we've had new items on the menu they would never have tried, but because they see Rob Feenie's name behind it, they're willing to."

When it comes to determined innovation, Jaffray offers the example of the margaritas they serve. Customers were accustomed to a typical frozen-slush margarita that came out of a machine. Cactus Club decided it was going to things differently, squeezing to order the limes for the drinks. "Initially it was a real battle. Customers were used to having slush from a machine. But we stuck with it." The customers came around, so much so that Cactus Club set the new standard for the drink in its market.

Innovation at the bar didn't stop at margarita slush. When tougher drinking-and-driving laws were introduced in British Columbia in 2010, Cactus Club revamped its beverage offerings with new low-alcohol (and zero-alcohol) cocktails, beer, and wine. And while making a margarita a different way may not sound like a major case of corporate innovation, it illustrates Cactus Club's determination to do things differently when it is convinced it's where the market needs to go, in order to keep the chain on the leading edge. In an industry where many competitors are followers, adopting new trends only after they have emerged elsewhere, Cactus Club is a true leader, getting ahead of the pack and innovating and creating anticipation.

Cactus Club is not playing catch-up with the customer's changing tastes. "We go where the customer doesn't even know they want to be yet," says Jaffray. It's a much different approach than anticipating a customer's future tastes. Cactus Club creates those tastes and leads the customer to them. "A lot of ideas require experimentation before we figure it out. But if we really believe in something as an organization, most of the time the customer will too."

● ● ●

The task of getting consumers to try an innovation out of their comfort zone is well known at SiriusXM Canada, whose story has been one of relentless innovation in both technology and the strategies for bringing that technology to market.

"When you look at what innovation has meant for us, you have to recognize that we had to innovate everything about our business," says Mark Redmond, president and CEO of SiriusXM Canada. "There has been huge innovation through the first ten years, and especially through the last three years. The technology of putting satellites in the air to deliver our content in a mobile market was the first part of innovations. There were hundreds of millions, billions of dollars spent to make satellite technology work on a North American platform. Then there was the innovation of creating all the content, a library of music in New York and Washington, servers containing every imaginable type of music."

The innovations were in no small part achieved with the technology in the vehicles, the radio unit and antenna, which has to satisfy a 90 percent reception quality. It also must be compatible with different climates and geographies. Innovation has extended down to the integrated circuits of chip technology, along with the ground repeaters and compression required to deliver 120-plus channels to a vehicle moving through varied terrain and weather at highway speed, as well as to other applications such as recreational boats and portable radios.

Having accomplished all that, satellite radio still had to be packaged in a viable, innovative commercial application. Part of the solution was in the hardware: Receivers had to be made part of pre-installed equipment by automakers, just as AM/FM radios and then CD players and MP3 audio jacks and USB plugs became standard issue. And for the millions of existing vehicles, a "plug and play" aftermarket receiver had to be created that would meet the needs of a myriad of vehicle manufacturers and models. The product had to be commercialized in a way that would get it into a retail environment, down to the level of displays, in multiple distribution channels. And there had to be a subscriber model that satisfied the nature of the automobile industry and vehicle ownership. With vehicle ownership often turning over every few years, there had to be a way for the receiver identification to move seamlessly from one car owner to another.

But for all of that to happen, the basic value proposition of subscription-based satellite radio had to be established and a convincing argument made to the millions of potential customers in North America—customers who were only the latest generation in a series of generations who were accustomed to getting content for free from the pre-installed AM/FM radio in the dashboard of their car, the stereo tuner in their home, or the portable radio they listened to in a football stadium for play-by-play.

How do you get people to pay for something they already get for free? That was the essential conundrum of satellite radio. According to Redmond, "to succeed, satellite radio would need to provide a superior listening experience in comparison to free radio, with high-quality reception across the continent, digital quality sound, and the best content available anywhere."

The satellite radio business model, says Redmond, is not dissimilar from that of cable and satellite television. "When cable TV launched, critics said 'There's no way people will pay for more

TV channels.' Then all of a sudden this one-hundred-channel universe appeared. Now people can't live without it because they were given an option that was significantly better than what they had. I think we've proven that consumers are willing to pay $15 a month for audio entertainment that is measurably superior to what they can get for free."

SiriusXM Canada utilizes satellite distribution technology that was pioneered and perfected by Sirius and XM Satellite Radio's forerunners in the United States more than a decade ago. Two XM satellites, called "Rock" and "Roll," were launched in 2001; Sirius followed suit and was broadcasting in 2002. Both companies traded on the NASDAQ.

With these proprietary satellites already in orbit, it was up to the Canadian companies to create a viable market proposition north of the border. In 2003, Canada's regulator, the CRTC, awarded its first satellite radio licence to Canadian Satellite Radio Holdings, parent of XM. A second licence was awarded in 2005 to Sirius Canada. Sirius Canada and XM Canada competed aggressively to establish factory-installation agreements with automakers and to make their aftermarket satellite radio products available in consumer electronics retailers across Canada. The companies also invested heavily in launching new Canadian channels that offered music from emerging Canadian artists and live sports and news. Sirius Canada was recognized as one of Canada's Best Managed Companies for the first time in 2008.

Following the merger of Sirius and XM in the United States in 2007, a merger was announced in November 2010 between Sirius Canada and XM Canada. In June 2011, the deal was finalized and Sirius Canada and XM Canada came together under the corporate umbrella of XM Canada's parent, Canadian Satellite Radio Holdings, to operate as SiriusXM Canada. Total subscribers surpassed two million in October 2011, making it one of Canada's largest media companies. Although it trades on the Toronto Stock Exchange (TSX), its current public float is less than 5 percent, so the company continues to qualify for the Best Managed Companies awards program.

SiriusXM Canada has capitalized on the fact that listeners are mobile, moving between the listening areas of land-based transmission towers that define where a conventional radio station's customer base is located. Freed from the restrictions of local broadcast licences, satellite radio focuses instead on delivering as large an array of content as receiver technology can manage and allows subscribers to choose what they want to listen to, regardless of location. They can drive across the country without having to change the channel.

For satellite radio, content is key. As Redmond stresses, "Content is the heart and soul of what we do. More than offering commercial-free music, it is our ability to offer niche channels and programming that sets satellite radio apart from commercial radio, MP3 players, and Internet radio." In addition to music channels for decades and genres, SiriusXM Canada has channels dedicated to specific artists including Pearl Jam, Bruce Springsteen, Neil Diamond, Frank Sinatra, and Jimmy Buffett (via "Radio Margaritaville"). Offerings include exclusive live sports play-by-play from the NFL, CFL, NHL and MLB, branded talk (including Howard Stern), entertainment and comedy channels, as well as news. Where standard network broadcasting models require programming to cast wide demographic nets, even within certain formats, satellite radio has taken the innovative approach of offering thinly sliced, highly targeted channel content in one comprehensive package, thus creating a net package of broad appeal.

SiriusXM Canada has also innovated in the way it has simplified its offering to consumers. It differs from typical cable and satellite television providers in that it has no complex menu of entertainment packages. For one monthly subscription fee, listeners receive access to more than 120 channels delivering an array of options in comedy, sports, music, news, and entertainment. Seamlessness of service, in both technology and content, is fundamental to the product offering. And SiriusXM Canada has adopted a simple subscription payment method: Customers choose a subscription term, and the monthly fee is automatically charged to a credit card account.

SiriusXM Canada has developed a partner model to enhance its own content offerings. The company is allied with CBC/Radio-Canada, Rogers Media, and the Weather Network (operated by Pelmorex Media Inc., a Best Managed Gold Standard company) to supplement the programming produced in its Toronto studio. Key distribution partners include a network of more than 3500 retailers nationwide, including Best Buy, Walmart, Future Shop, and The Source.

While the company addresses specialty markets like trucks and boats, its growth engine continues to be the automotive market. It has made great strides in having receivers pre-installed as original equipment in new vehicles. From a handful of manufacturers and models in 2006, the install base for Sirius and XM has grown significantly over the years, and the company now has agreements in place with every major Canadian manufacturer.

Having receivers pre-installed in new vehicles is critical to expanding the subscriber base. Potential customers no longer have to consider purchasing an aftermarket unit and having it installed; the technology cost is contained within the vehicle purchase. For vehicle manufacturers, offering the receiver technology as standard equipment on certain models makes satellite radio a competitive differentiator for their own product, rather than a retail aftermarket option.

With an increasing installed base, SiriusXM Canada is also exploring ways to use its satellite and Internet distribution infrastructure to extend its product offerings. The Sirius platform is expanding options with mobile listening apps for iPhone, Android and BlackBerry smartphones, portable satellite radio products like the Stiletto 2, and the Synergi Internet Radio device for the home. The company also expects to introduce tabular and graphic weather displays and traffic conditions. Redmond says the technology will even make it possible for subscribers to access movie listings, gas prices, and stock market quotes in real time.

SiriusXM Canada is thus pursuing a compelling avenue of innovation: capitalizing on the essential capabilities of its core technology to broaden its product offering in a way that logically extends its brand. The company is extending its product range into services that could significantly increase the appeal of the technology beyond the core target market of commuters who spend about an hour or more at the wheel every day. Content remains the core of what SiriusXM Canada offers. Now, the content is innovating beyond the initial appeal of commercial-free radio.

"The success of our business depends on how well and how quickly we can leverage key innovations to continually improve the customer experience," says Redmond. "We rely on technological innovation to keep pace."

• • •

"Innovation" in business tends to conjure images of patentable technology: products that have some unique engineered features that qualify them as intellectual property. Newterra is one company that has turned to such product innovation to differentiate itself in the marketplace, but its approach to innovation isn't limited to designing or acquiring unique products that can find shelter from commodifying competition in patent documents. It's another company that has embraced a culture devoted to change, which, like Cactus Club, has extended to defying expectations of how a business in its industry is supposed to function.

Bruce Lounsbury co-founded Newterra (which until March 2012 was known as Calco Environmental Group) in 1992, and as president and CEO he is responsible for its strategic direction. Its operating companies design, manufacture, commission, and support turnkey solutions for soil remediation and the treatment of air and water in industrial applications. In the first eight years of its existence, Lounsbury says "we were tending to focus on manufacturing systems and equipment, largely to other people's design and specifications. We could do technical things, like mechanical and electrical design, but around 2000 we peaked out in our ability to grow doing business that way. We started to look at how we could bring more technology to the marketplace."

Newterra became a company that embraced innovation as the key to its competitive advantage. Much of the innovation has involved new technologies. But it has also involved new ways of thinking about the process of satisfying and engaging the customer, and it has sometimes defied the prevailing wisdom about how a company like it should deploy assets.

Newterra continues to grow by focusing on technological solutions for environmental issues, delivered through collaboration with partners and customers. Its strategic emphasis is on solutions sales in the $50,000 to $2 million range. Under the group umbrella are the operating companies Maple Leaf Environmental Equipment, Filter Innovations, Steel Services, and Pacwill Environmental. For partnerships, it looks to the best companies and people in each industry segment and has used strategic acquisition to complement its steady, organic growth.

Newterra has found increasing success in the waste water market, treating "black" (sewage) and "grey" (shower and sink) water with its Membrane Bio Reactor (MBR) Systems. It has been especially successful in the mining camp market, petroleum exploration, and the agrifood business. It is also finding significant opportunities to provide complete customer solutions in landfill sites, where gas recovery and monitoring systems, along with leachate collection and treatment, form a niche for which its approach of providing engineered, turnkey systems is ideally suited.

Where technology is concerned, Newterra has realized that there are two levels of innovation to be exploited. One is what Lounsbury calls "the big steps." These are the innovations most people think of when they imagine advances in technology. They are significant, patentable inventions that can be game-changers in business. The big steps do factor in Newterra's success. These have been acquired or brought to the marketplace through partnering or business acquisitions as well as through the creation of new intellectual property.

But there is another world of innovation, involving incremental improvements—a world that many businesses do not even recognize as existing. Those small steps in improving an existing technology or process add up, and they are recognized by Canada's Scientific Research & Incremental Development (SR&ED) tax incentive program, the single largest federal source of support for industrial R&D, which rewards innovation through tax credits and/or cash refunds.

"Deloitte helped us quite a bit with SR&ED," says Lounsbury. "We were able to recognize how we were making incremental improvements in a process. We were now getting funding because we were creating new knowledge. At any point in time now, we have two to three initiatives under way to protect incremental intellectual property. It might be a new design for a clarification system that takes clever advantage of hydraulics, for example."

Companies that stake their competitive advantage on innovation have to be prepared to defend the uniqueness of their offerings. "As we grew from our early days as a manufacturing and packaging company, we became a systems integrator and solutions provider," says Lounsbury. "As you move down that path, bringing your own solutions to customers' problems, protecting the solutions becomes important."

Protecting innovation raises the spectre of constant legal actions to defend patents. "We're the best in the world in small to mid-size MBR, in the design of membrane systems and grey water treatment, and there has been an element of copying going on in membrane technology," says Lounsbury. "We also have a welding process which, if push came to shove, we'd defend. Both these areas of intellectual property are critical for us, as they set us apart in the marketplace."

But Lounsbury says protection of innovation is far more nuanced than launching lawsuits. "It's not that you necessarily have to defend against competitors, suing people for infringement of intellectual property rights. It's about creating the impression among customers and competitors that an innovation is something you own and do. It lets the marketplace know that you have protected technology and the best brain power."

While Newterra is recognized for its technology innovations, Lounsbury stresses that innovation cannot stop at engineering drawings and software code. "There's more innovation in business than people think. If all you're thinking about is the next major innovation in your industry, you're going to miss a lot of things in much more mundane areas."

For Newterra, innovation has included project management. It has rethought the workflow process in search of efficiencies. "We get more information now from customers early, more buy-in and sign-off. We get them to be much more part of the process at the beginning. If we do things in a vacuum without their buy-in, our chance of delivering well is significantly lower."

Newterra also took a fresh look at the factors crucial to a project's success. "One of them is delivery, especially where major fabricated components are concerned," says Lounsbury. There had been a tremendous amount of outsourcing in Newterra's industry, as companies withdrew from or avoided manufacturing. But because of its analysis, Newterra bucked the trend and invested in manufacturing, acquiring a steel fabricating unit, which operates as Steel Services.

"We got into the steel business so we could control that part of our own business," says Lounsbury. "Outside investors would look at us and ask: 'Why is a water treatment business involved in metal fabrication?' But they've gone from thinking of recommending we shed a 'non-core' process to recognizing that it's mission critical."

Steel Services has paid additional dividends. This division purchased and installed a high-capacity laser steel cutting machine, which has allowed Newterra to participate in the "renaissance repatriation" of the production of heavy, high-accuracy steel products in North America. Newterra's million-dollar investment is the first of its kind in North America, thus providing the company with a competitive advantage, positioning it to access markets in manufacturing that it has otherwise been unable to pursue, including tank manufacture and steel components for the alternative energy, waste heat recovery, and water processing industries.

Bruce Lounsbury believes the lessons Newterra has learned about innovation have broad application in businesses of all kinds. "Don't be blinded by the notion that innovation involves big things," he advises. "Think of the small as well as the big. Innovation exists in all sorts of boring stuff that makes you much better. Most of us are not going to hit home runs. But there are a lot of things that make the difference between failure and success, and between being successful and being very successful."

• • •

The companies discussed in this chapter demonstrate that innovation requires an organization to embrace a culture of change, of risk-taking. But the idea that change is "risky" is counterintuitive to these companies. To them, not embracing change, not striving for innovation, risks failure.

Many companies find themselves changing their products or services because they have no choice. After all, necessity is the mother of invention. The companies we have met innovate because change defines and delivers their market advantage. They believe in their innovative propositions, reject the idea that the standard model of their industry is the one to be adhered to, and are confident that the customer is capable of recognizing the value of difference where there is measurable improvement and novelty. They also know that seemingly small improvements can end up being much bigger than they would appear. Where effective leadership inspires a constant drive to achieve the small, there is a culture of change throughout the organization that moves the entire enterprise forward.

# 8

# TECHNOLOGY: FASTER, BETTER, CHEAPER

In 1998, the Bragg Group's communications company, EastLink, became the first Canadian cable company to break the traditional "telco" monopoly by offering local telephone service in direct competition with traditional phone companies. While EastLink used a coaxial cable network, it ran true circuit-switched telephony—voice over Internet protocol (VOIP) would come later. But while it had managed to adapt a coaxial network to telephone service, it hit a tech wall when it came to charging for the new service. Because its account system was designed for cable television service, which was based on flat rates, EastLink found it had a major limitation in its existing billing capability. Unlike the telcos, it had no way to offer the "*" feature options in the way that customers of established telephone companies were used to paying for. The telcos billed on a per-use basis, and the charges for the use of a popular feature like *69 (to identify the last call received) could add up.

Were it left to IT experts, a company like EastLink might have been compelled to introduce a new billing platform with a "*" feature menu of its own, in order to avoid leaving customer revenues on the table. Instead, EastLink accepted the limitation of its existing system as it went to market with the new service.

"We fell into offering everything for a flat rate," says CEO Lee Bragg. In the process, the company created a compelling perception of value for customers who had been accustomed to pay-as-you go features.

"It taught us simpler is better," says Bragg. "Our technology was special, but it's how we deployed it for the customers that was most important."

● ● ●

Whenever "innovation" is discussed, people routinely look to technology for examples. But as we saw in Chapter 7, "Innovation: How Trendsetting Organizations Embrace a Culture of Change," defying the conventions of a casual dining experience, as in the case of Cactus Club, has nothing to do with software or engineering breakthroughs. Technology can be an important aspect of innovation, but it remains a subject in its own right. In this chapter we meet companies that are using technology to increase their competitive advantage, changing the way they interact with customers and enhancing the capabilities of their workforce while improving productivity. The Bragg Group's EastLink is an interesting variation on that main theme. Although its communication products are built on leading-edge technology, the company has learned— even if it meant falling into a solution—that particular technology products are not what it is ultimately selling. Like other companies in this chapter, Bragg understands that the drivers determining the successful deployment of technology often have nothing to do with being first-to-market with "cool stuff."

Best Managed Companies see technology as an opportunity

rather than a new wrinkle in the cost of doing business. As we explained in Chapter 3, "Branding and Marketing: the Product an Experience, Not a Thing," they have turned to social media for brand building and to data analytics and enterprise resource planning (ERP) systems for greater visibility of operations and market opportunities. A few years ago, only large companies could implement major ERP systems. These systems have recently become more accessible to everyone, which is creating significant opportunities for enhancing performance for private companies in addition to the public giants.

Data, in fact, is becoming so critical to competitiveness that we expect efforts to harness "big data"—the digital mountain of largely unstructured and unsifted data lurking in corporate systems—will experience accelerating growth and market penetration, as traditional analytics tools can't always keep up with the information being collected. By the end of 2012, we predict that more than 90 percent of Fortune 500 companies will have some sort of big-data initiative underway in an attempt to manage their overflowing data warehouses and move insights closer to real time and closer to the end customer. While the early adopters of big-data technologies were Internet companies, the fast followers are likely to be those in the public sector, financial services, retail, entertainment, and media industries.

Best Managed Companies approach technology from the perspective of how it can make them more effective, and in this book we see other examples of this—in dashboard reporting and balance-sheet forecasting, for example, and in building strong IT backbones that enable smooth acquisitions or highly efficient supply-chain management. Because these companies understand the importance of technology in an array of applications, they invest in it consistently and well over the long term, even as competitors are making spending cuts. In fact, private-equity companies have been telling us that one of the first litmus tests they apply to a prospective investment is what type of dashboard reporting and other IT measures are being used. This demonstrates to the private-equity companies whether or not "management gets it." And as we explain, mid-size companies are investing in internal technology capabilities and talent, in order to create the custom tools they need when off-the-shelf solutions either don't exist or fail to measure up to their standards.

● ● ●

The Bragg Group followed an unusual trajectory to becoming a leading-edge provider of communications services for consumers and businesses. The family enterprise started out in food in 1968, when Lee Bragg's father, John, founded Oxford Frozen Foods and a number of associated frozen food processing and blueberry farming businesses in Cumberland County, Nova Scotia. The Bragg Group is still in the food business, but in 1970 it diversified into communications when it was issued one of the first CRTC licences for cable television, which it introduced initially to Amherst, Nova Scotia, under the EastLink banner. Lee Bragg says the family enterprise's roots in the food industry are evident in its approach to running EastLink. "We come from a very cost-focused industry, and we brought that mentality into a newly opened industry."

A series of strategic acquisitions has allowed EastLink to become the fifth largest (and the largest privately held) cable company in Canada. In February 2011, the Bragg Group ventured outside Canada for the first time with the purchase of Bermuda's Cable and Wireless (Bermuda) Holdings Ltd. (CWBH), a

121-year-old Bermuda telecommunications operation with both residential and business customers.

EastLink has made new technology a key differentiator, spending $650 million over the past seven years in capital programs as it has set competitive benchmarks in cable television, high-speed Internet, and local and long-distance telephone service. In 2000, it was the first company anywhere in North America to bundle services on a single bill, with a "triple play" for local telephone, Internet, and cable television service. The company continues to invest in the necessary technology to deliver new products, including digital TV, high-definition (HD), 3D and OnDemand programming, and Multi-Room DVR, all while upholding its reputation as one of North America's providers of the fastest Internet service available.

EastLink used to think of itself as a network/technology company. That has changed. "We do use technology, and we've had a better network than some competitors," says Lee Bragg. "Everybody's technology can improve, though, and so we need to be a customer relationship company. We can't live on the fact that we have a better mousetrap. We focus everything we do on what can best satisfy customers."

With Internet products, he notes, there can be "all kinds of peripheral bells and whistles. We just concentrate on delivering speed, a good, reliable, quick connection. The technology question for us is: How do we make the network perform as best we can? Technology is not there to fool customers into making something seem more complicated than it is."

That philosophy has been expressed most emphatically in EastLink's approach to pricing. "Make the price the price. With video and HD channels, we said, 'Let's get them on the network, and package them in an easy manner.'" Bragg says the company is taking the same approach with the cellular service it plans to introduce in late 2012—"simplify things." The benefits accrue to EastLink in a far less complex relationship with its customers. "Our technology is special, but it's how we've deployed it for the customers that is important." Offering basic bundled and flat-rate services greatly simplifies the diversity and volume of calls being handled by a contact centre, eliminating the problems of customers trying to turn a myriad of features on or off from one billing period to another. "Simplicity reduces your costs and makes you more efficient and effective," Bragg explains.

Lee Bragg is an admirer of Apple. "It really gets the customer. They get the technology and the customer." Its consumer products work intuitively, without expecting users to be software engineers. He wants EastLink's offerings to meet the same standards.

"We like technology," he emphasizes, "but just because something is there that can be done doesn't mean the customer is going to understand it. I like the 20/80 rule. Twenty percent of what's available generally is going to satisfy 80 percent of customers."

EastLink, he says, is focused on answering the question: What is the customer's problem and how do we solve it? "We have to be in the relationship business, not the technology business. It's a simple business, really. Figure out what the customer needs and deliver it."

● ● ●

Figuring out what the customer needs and delivering it has been the hallmark of the way another Best Managed Companies winner from Atlantic Canada—Maritime Travel—has deployed technology. The travel industry is highly competitive, sometimes brutally so. In the 1990s, more than a few small business people lost their savings investing in travel agency franchises, not understanding that a love of travel in and of itself does not translate into a viable business model. Fierce competition among airlines and online discount services have made it harder than ever for the typical travel agency to hold its ground and persuade the consumer of the value proposition of its services.

Maritime Travel, founded with a single office in 1949, has been reaping accolades and growing, both geographically and in revenues and profits, throughout a turbulent period in the travel business. Maritime Travel is present in virtually every niche, from airline charter travel to wedding planning to last-minute vacation package deals. It services consumer and business travellers alike through three channels. It has a network of travel agencies in ninety-six locations (and counting). Most of them operate as Maritime Travel, with nineteen locations in Newfoundland and Labrador branded LeGrow's Travel, and several in Quebec and northern New Brunswick known as Voyages Maritime. A second channel is its Web presence that allows direct online booking by consumers, including by smartphone. Its third channel is its call centre, staffed by what Maritime calls "counsellors."

"We almost look at ourselves as a technology company rather than a travel company," says president Gary Gaudry. Technology is harnessed to meet several intertwined goals. Foremost, product innovations enabled by technology differentiate Maritime Travel in the marketplace, providing customers (particularly business travellers) with value-added services in account management as well as in the quality of their service experience. Technology also impacts the employee in a positive manner: Not only are they more effective in servicing customers, their job satisfaction (as measured, for example, by "engagement") increases as they are better equipped to perform tasks that they know set the company apart. The travel industry is ultimately about helping people, and the more productively helpful employees feel, the better they feel about their jobs.

A backbone of the travel industry is the global distribution system (GDS), also known as a computer reservation system (CRS), a number of which were created globally by technology companies to consolidate information from the many different suppliers of travel services—initially airlines, but eventually hotels, car rental companies, and the like. A GDS is how a travel agency accesses many disparate elements of a client's trip, providing options, handling the bookings, and issuing tickets and receipts. While GDS remains a chief technology resource of travel companies, airlines and other suppliers have developed their own direct-to-consumer booking options, particularly on the Web, and not all airline travel information is distributed through a GDS. Air Canada's discount Tango service, as well as discounted "consolidator fares," are not available through GDS.

In 1997, perhaps 1 percent of travellers in the United States, for example, were booking travel online. That figure had increased to 11 percent by 2002 and has only continued to grow. The rise of direct Web-based booking of hotels, airline tickets, and rental cars has been a technology challenge to the standard travel-agency business model that Maritime Travel for one has met with technology of its own.

"More people are preferring to book on websites rather than with the old GDS systems," says Gaudry, an observation that applies as much to travel agency staff as it does to consumers. Maritime Travel has built atop GDS a Web interface called Sales Desk that its staff (both in agency offices and online) can employ to access its data through simple point-and-click methods rather than having to master and then use time-consuming GDS codes and protocols.

Introduced in 2004, Sales Desk has been continuously refined, with new features and capabilities. It can generate an Apollo Client Statement, an all-in-one document incorporating itinerary, invoice, and eTicket. The document is fully customizable by Maritime Travel, it can draw information from a variety of sources to build a more easily readable PDF document, and it's available in both official languages. This technology is built on the new SQL reporting services and is available to the company's agents with a mouse click. The reservation system used to force agents to print documents, but they now have the choice of either printing or e-mailing the document. The document also contains several quick-link items to Web check-in, online itinerary, and the individual counsellor's e-mail when the document is provided electronically. In 2011, Maritime Travel added a hot link to Trip-It, so itineraries can be quickly added to the customer's Trip-It account or viewed on TravelPort's ViewTrip website with mobile devices.

Customer calls are also no longer routed to the first available counsellor. Customers can now specify a particular counsellor as their representative and have all their transactions made through him or her. For the customer and counsellor alike, a personal relationship can be established that overcomes the anonymity of call-centre support and transforms the counsellor into a virtual travel agent, lacking only the bricks-and-mortar office.

With customers having so many online booking options before them, Maritime Travel has turned to technology to increase its value proposition, particularly with business travellers. One area that drove particularly beneficial change was credit card reconciliation. Maritime Travel developed a client account statement that allows businesses who use its booking services to reconcile travel expenses charged to corporate credit cards. These clients then asked if Maritime Travel could take reconciliation down to the individual department level, and it was able to do that as well. In 2011, Maritime Travel offered reconciliation by traveller for individuals who were charging their trips to personal cards while on company business.

Another business-friendly feature Maritime Travel has developed is an unused ticket tracker, responding to a gap in the product offerings available. Third-party products offered on the markets were only capturing unused tickets booked on GDS or reservation systems. With over half of tickets now being booked through a website portal, many unused tickets were not being captured by existing tools. Maritime Travel thus built its own unused ticket tracker, which captures both GDS and Web-booked unused tickets.

Maritime Travel's innovations have been aimed at increasing both client and employee satisfaction. "You don't want your people spending their time doing the booking," says Gaudry. "You want them to be spending their time with the customer." As sophisticated as the solutions are, he expects technology employed by staff to be simple to use. "It drives me crazy when someone says, 'Well, we just need to train someone more and they'll know how to do it.'" Like Lee Bragg of EastLink, Gaudry admires the standard set by Apple. "Stuff should be intuitive. Does someone with an iPhone need training to know how to use it? We want to hire people who are good salespeople, not technology experts." The technology motto he adheres to is: "It's faster, easier, better. Not slower, harder, worse."

● ● ●

Technology as deployed by a company like Maritime Travel is fundamentally transparent to consumers. When they're booking airline tickets through Maritime's website, they know they're dealing through Maritime with service providers and in fact are looking for Maritime's help to do so. The consumer experience is far less obvious in shopping for the products of Chaussures Régence

of Quebec City, but the technology-enabled process is no less dedicated to making online purchasing efficient and satisfying.

Consider an American woman shopping for new boots, who
visits the website of the U.S. retailer Nordstrom's and selects the
Blondo brand, narrowing her choice to the Valente waterproof
style. She chooses size 7—one of thirteen options between 5.5
and 13—in the colour "café." The order page gives her the option
of picking up her new boots in a bricks-and-mortar Nordstrom's
outlet, but she wants them delivered to her house and proceeds with
completing the online order.

As far as this consumer knows, the order she has placed is on its
way from a Nordstrom's warehouse somewhere. In fact, the entire
electronic transaction has occurred, via Nordstrom's Web presence,
between the consumer and the boots' manufacturer, Chaussures
Régence. Even had she placed the order for pickup at a store near
her, the order would have been placed directly from the website
with Chaussures Régence, which would take care of fulfillment
from a new U.S. warehouse.

"The consumer always thinks the order comes from
Nordstrom's," says Chaussures Régence's president, Christian
Bergeron. "It's not a complicated issue, but it's a matter of putting
the technology in place to make it easier for our customer." For
Chaussures Régence, that customer is the retailer, and it has worked
with Nordstrom's and other purveyors like Zappos and Shoe.com
(both of which are exclusively online and have no bricks-and-
mortar outlets) to develop an electronic data interchange (EDI)
system that makes online shopping simple for the store as well as
for the consumer.

EDI systems link the computer data systems of different
companies. The advantages of Chaussures Régence's new EDI
fulfillment system, called Drop Ship, are widely shared. For the

consumer, there is speed of fulfillment, with no required inter-mediary steps between retailer and manufacturer. The consumer also has access to the entire catalogue of the manufacturer, which is a considerable asset to the manufacturer as well as the retailer. Chaussures Régence doesn't have to persuade retail buyers to order and stock a particular quantity of models. It can be sure that its entire product line is being seen by potential buyers, with orders just a click away.

"What people want on the Internet," says Bergeron, "is to have a wide range of offerings. Zappos, for example, has the ability to show hundreds of thousands of products on its website, compared to hundreds in a regular store. People who have a store as well as a Web presence often make the mistake of having the same thing online as they do in the store." The Web, says Bergeron, doesn't require a retailer to have a fixed customer identity and to limit the offerings accordingly. "Online, customers want variety and choice, and you want to show all the shoes you have. Dress shoes, athletic shoes, boots ..."

For retailers, there is an enormous advantage to Drop Ship not having to worry about warehousing and inventory. They set online sales objectives according to whatever they hope to sell, so there is no commitment in pre-ordering inventory and stocking it some-where. Warehousing is Chaussures Régence's responsibility, and the new U.S. warehouse meets the U.S. retailers' preference that the customer receives a purchase from an American address. And, of course, the retailer doesn't have to worry about fulfilling the shipping order.

For Chaussures Régence, EDI means that with smart data analytics enabled by its new Customer Relationship Management (CRM) software, it can develop a precise image of how individual models are selling day to day and by different retailers (and customer regions, since it is handling shipping). Its own manufacturing can be much leaner and more responsive to demands; consumer behaviour is real-time and reveals trends that can help influence designs and product mix. Such data is vital because 75 percent of its fashion collection is updated every year.

The introduction of Drop Ship has been one more step in the evolution of Chaussures Régence, whose roots as a shoe manufacturer reach back to 1910. Today it views itself as a company devoted to design, sales, and marketing, competing in a global environment. Manufacturing was transferred to China in 2005, with a staff of twelve placed there to oversee costs and quality control. It views strategic alliances with its retail clients and distributors, and the exchange of information with them, as key elements of its business plan.

Christian Bergeron began working at his father's company when he was in his teens. At age twenty-four in 1986, he joined the company full-time after earning a degree in business administration with a concentration in finance and information technology. "My first job out of school was at my dad's company," he recalls. "He said to me, 'Your job is to take care of computers.'" Since then, computers—software, at least—have acquired an increasing importance in the company's operations.

"I developed our first IT system, 100 percent for us," he says. Programming is no longer his main concern, as he became president in 1992. Today, Chaussures Régence has its own IT team of three programmers. "We're developing our own tools in-house, and the people who work for us have the tools that fit their needs. They didn't come from another industry. The ideas come from our people, and we develop the tools with our own team." Good management, says Bergeron, "means helping everybody in the company do the best job they can by giving them the best tools.

In today's environment, that means giving them the necessary computer tools."

Technology is not what Chaussures Régence sells. Its product is footwear, and its revenues depend on quality and fashion. But technology has allowed the company to make the process of selling for its retail clients as efficient as possible. When Christian Bergeron assumed the presidency, sales were about $5 million annually. They are now up to $40 million. Drop Ship has turned into a shoe that fits and that retail partners want to wear.

• • •

"I've always sold a technology-*enabled* service," says Jason Smith of Real Matters. "It's never just technology."

For some two decades, Smith has been developing and deploying technology-enabled services for the financial services market, the latest of which is Real Matters of Markham, Ontario, a Best Managed Companies winner. Smith has excelled at identifying pressure points of value, principally in the cost structure of mortgage processing.

"Traditionally, banks spend about $2200 processing a mortgage," he explains. Smith started out looking for a way to make the process more efficient, and his initial solution was at the point of sale, with the consumer application in the office of mortgage brokers. He provided an automated software application, and his business model was to give the software to the mortgage brokers for free; the banks that secured a mortgage through his software would be the ones to pay Smith on each transaction.

"Then the Internet came around," he recalls. And so there was a new business model, with a new technology solution. With consumers flocking to the online world, he built the first consumer mortgage-shopping site anywhere in the world—for Canadians. "The challenge was that the bank just wanted you to fax in a mortgage application. Banks were still so manual at that time. So instead we applied the new Internet technology to business-to-business. We had enormous success going there to reduce the banks' mortgage processing costs."

The Canadian market, however, proved to be too small. Growth would have to come in the United States. "I went to the States and asked: Where is the real pain in the mortgage process? It was in appraisals." Smith decided the appraisal business could be automated. He bought property-tax data from offices across the United States and created a searchable database. For about $25, a lender could arrive at an appraisal based on assessed and neighbourhood valuations rather than sending out an appraiser. He built the business up to a 60 percent market share of automated appraisals before selling it.

His company, Basis100, developed lines of business that included lending solutions for consumer credit, mortgage origination and processing, data warehousing and analytics solutions for automated property valuations, property data-warehousing, data products and analytics support, and capital markets solutions for fixed-income trading. Basis100 enlisted over 1700 U.S. mortgage vendors to use its automated valuation services for residential mortgages, and established customer relationships with twenty-three of the top twenty-five mortgage lenders in the U.S. market. Smith sold Basis100 in 2003 (its U.S. division was sold separately in 2004). It's still going strong, being used by the Canadian banks, for example.

At that point, Jason Smith considered himself done with building and divesting himself of technology companies. "I thought I was just going to go fly fishing. But I missed working with smart people." He started talking with bankers in Canada, the United States, and the United Kingdom, again looking for a pain point that technology could resolve. It turned out to be in home appraising, the cost bottleneck he had tried to resolve with his last company.

Smith knew there was an essential weakness in his last creation. Using tax databases to reach an appraisal might work for a suburb of cookie-cutter homes, but automated valuation models had trouble when they encountered older neighbourhoods with mixed housing stock, for example. "These models couldn't consistently appraise about 50 percent of the housing stock," he notes.

There was still an important role for appraisers in the field. The problem the mortgage industry had was that appraising was their second-highest processing cost. But appraisers had problems of their own. Lending institutions outsourced appraising to appraisal companies, and appraisers were getting squeezed financially in the way the per-appraisal spend (about $400) was divided.

The appraisers' problems were ultimately the banks' problems as well. "The banks were unhappy with the vendors who were getting their appraisers," says Smith. Whenever professionals are under-paid, the better ones are driven from the business altogether and the ones left behind are less experienced, less reliable, and under increasing pressure to do their work in less time, which generally means less thoroughly.

Having last created a technology product that was designed to eliminate the need for on-site appraisals, Smith now could see that appraisers themselves needed a supportive technology product. His new company, Real Matters, created a virtual marketplace, Solidifi, on the company's cloud-based redihive platform, where appraisers could set their own fees and also receive feedback on how they were performing in that marketplace relative to their peers. "We thought that if we could work on a fraction of an appraisal's $400 and pass along more to the appraiser, then appraisers would be better paid and more reliable. Wow, were we right."

Real Matters built Solidifi for the North American market, but initially launched it only in Canada in 2006. "It went very well. The banks also wanted underwriting scorecards. They were screening for better quality and faster service in appraising, and for that you have to bring technology to bear." Thus, Real Matters extended its services to the banks themselves. At the same time, the Solidifi service to appraisers expanded to provide a workflow tool in location management and scheduling—what Real Matters calls "loading the truck" with appointments in a specific geographic area.

When Real Matters decided it was ready to take its services to the U.S. market, the housing market was in a meltdown. "We saw that as a once-in-a-lifetime opportunity to win a big market share. The tough part was finding the top appraisers. In five-and-a-half months, we raised capital, doubled the delivery team, landed a very large bank as a client, and signed up several thousand appraisers. It absolutely took off."

Technology, not surprisingly, has been the greatest differentiator for Jason Smith in his business ventures that have culminated in Real Matters. "It has allowed me to work on a cost structure that lets me turn a business upside-down. We run the whole U.S. operation in Markham." Technology has also allowed him to create region-sensitive services in a highly localized industry. "Real estate is a regional market, with local laws and compliance issues." The last thing you want to create in a technology, Smith advises, is "a lowest-common-denominator approach" that fails to address critical market differences.

• • •

Jason Smith of Real Matters is a strong believer in companies retaining technology as a core competency, rather than outsourcing it. "If technology is not one of your core competencies," he cautions, "then you are missing out, as the devil is in the details." Developing technology in-house is a solution companies often resort to rather than set out to do. "Our goal is to have a third party supply us, not to build it ourselves," says Gary Gaudry of Maritime Travel. "But we find that not everything we need is out there. We don't limit ourselves to 'travel specific' technology. We look at the best technology out there for the job."

Conestoga Cold Storage found itself in a similar position when it set out to bring robotics and automation to its warehouse and distribution business. "We've always looked for an off-the-shelf solution, and usually the ones we found weren't robust and reliable enough," says Gavin Sargeant, vice-president of automation.

Conestoga Cold Storage offers more than twenty-seven million cubic feet of storage at warehousing and blast-freezing facilities in Kitchener and Mississauga in Ontario, Calgary in Alberta, and Vaudreuil-Dorion and Dorval in the Montreal area. Certified by the Canadian Food Inspection Agency, it can distribute goods around North America as well as to the European Union. Companies like M&M Meat Shops, Janes Family Foods, and Maple Leaf Consumer Foods rely on Conestoga Cold Storage to handle enormous volumes of product that need to be safely stored in a cold environment (although it handles non-frozen goods as well).

Conestoga Cold Storage's transformation into a technology-driven company began in 1980, when the company was handling dry packaging and had not yet moved into the cold-storage market. It wanted to introduce automated storage and retrieval (ASR) to the handling of customer pallets. When it couldn't find an acceptable solution off-the-shelf, the company developed its own capabilities.

It built its own high-rise building, designed its own robotic pallet-handling cranes, and created its own ASR software to run the cranes. It became the first cold-storage company in North America with ASR robotic pallet handling, and it is still the only one in Canada with the technology.

Once Conestoga Cold Storage had gone the do-it-yourself route, there was no turning back. "We manufacture our robotic cranes and buildings in-house," says Sargeant. "We also handle software internally. We really look aggressively at finding a solution rather than doing it ourselves, but we have high expectations for reliability, and outside systems have not met those expectations."

In 2006, the company built a customized research and development facility to design, build, and test its innovations. The initiative was part of a multi-year commitment to achieving an ambitious goal of implementing "auto-picking" in its warehouses. Conestoga Cold Storage had begun to investigate the possibility seriously in 2003.

Conestoga Cold Storage wanted to achieve automated case-level order picking. A typical customer pallet has one hundred cases of goods. In serving as a distribution centre, Conestoga has to fulfill orders that require only parts of different pallets—a few cases from this pallet, a few from another one—and they can be in different sized boxes. Building up a pallet is normally a manual exercise with a pallet jack. With an automated system, Conestoga could break orders down to a few cases from different pallets with robotics. "It's designed for product that is difficult to handle and expensive," says Conestoga's president, Greg Laurin. "These products are heavy, and valuable, with a high security risk. And you want to remove as much labour as you can from a harsh environment."

The fully automated picking system, introduced in 2010 after several years of R&D, remains the first of its kind in Canada. Fully designed and developed in-house, the system has a picking capacity of more than thirty thousand cases per day. The system has driven out the productivity waste represented by time. The volume of work that a conventional system completes in twenty-four hours can now be achieved in only eight hours. In addition to drastically reducing the number of hours its employees spend in cold temperatures, it has increased picking accuracy to almost 100 percent.

The achievement of automated picking has been part of an over-arching drive to monitor every aspect of Conestoga Cold Storage's operations in the name of efficiency and profitability. Every piece of equipment in its warehouse is fitted with radio frequency (RF) computer terminals that direct and monitor product movement through every stage of the shipping and receiving process. Each transaction is recorded, and the information is directly linked back to the account details of the customer. This procedure, known as activity-based costing (ABC), allows Conestoga Cold Storage to precisely measure each client account for profitability and compare actual results to its original pricing predictions. The company has also incorporated warehouse data into its dashboard technology, displaying it on large monitors so that warehouse activity can be tracked and evaluated in real time.

Conestoga Cold Storage's achievements have not gone unnoticed in other industries. Having devoted years to creating its own technology solutions where off-the-shelf products were lacking, the company now finds other companies wondering if its innovations could solve their own problems. "There's been significant interest from material handling companies for the technology," says Laurin. The idea that Conestoga Cold Storage could turn its automation expertise into a revenue centre "is a consideration that has some potential."

• • •

For the companies we have discussed in this chapter, technology is not a one-off project aimed at a particular problem. The commitment to technology as a solutions provider and a competitive enabler is a core competency and is rooted deep in the corporate culture. Keeping it there requires discipline. "Committing to long term R&D is a challenge," says Greg Laurin of Conestoga Cold Storage, where automated warehouse picking took about seven years to design, perfect, and implement. "You need to stay focused on a project and keep it moving forward when it's not going to be used right away. If something isn't going into production immediately, it can fall behind."

At Real Matters, the central importance of technology is reflected in the fact that the chief technology officer (CTO) is not a support role. "Our CTO is probably the best salesperson in the organization," says Jason Smith. The CTO has to understand the true benefits of technology, he says, not the proverbial bells and whistles. Real Matters' CTO is integrated with the executive team. "Technology isn't a seat at the table. It's the centre of the table. The CTO's job is to align our developers with the business, to bring the real needs of the business forward to the developers. Nothing is more demotivating to a developer than if a project never launches or the customer never uses it."

And at the end of the day, the true value of technology is not measured by its "cool factor." The value is expressed through the metrics of productivity, customer satisfaction, and employee engagement.

Maritime Travel's people, says Gary Gaudry, are "the key to our business. On average they've been with us fifteen-plus years." Technology in turn is key to staff effectiveness, which is inseparable from their job satisfaction. Every year, Maritime Travel conducts an employee engagement survey. The staff scored 87 percent in 2011, "an incredible score," says Gaudry. "One of the key measures is if someone truly enjoys their day-to-day work. One way to achieve that is to have work processes that allow them to be as productive as possible. 'Great' processes that slow down our front line are not acceptable."

Perhaps one of the greatest benefits of technology is that companies that embrace it as a core competency also tend to embrace change. Technology is an adaptive response to unpredictability, but companies that are technology-savvy also create that unpredictability, to their competitive advantage.

As EastLink's Lee Bragg puts it, "We're nimble people. We *like* upheaval. We think it works to our advantage."

# 9

# SUSTAINABILITY: DOING THE RIGHT THINGS FOR CUSTOMERS AND COMMUNITIES

"If being green or sustainable costs more money, then that solution isn't sustainable itself," says Scott Jenkins, president of DIRTT, the Calgary-based firm that is radically changing the way buildings are constructed with its stylish and eco-friendly modular interiors. "It's the ethos of how we've built our business. We believe in changing a very conservative industry, but if we don't make a value proposition, we can't succeed."

DIRTT (an acronym for Doing It Right This Time) has been asking companies to rethink their approach to office space—to the way building interiors are designed, constructed, and redeployed over time. Its approach to modular design and manufacturing goes far beyond partitions that reject fixed studs and drywall.

DIRTT was founded in 2004 by Calgary entrepreneur Mogens Smed, who earned a 2010 Product Prize, presented by the American Society of Interior Design to an individual whose products or philosophy have contributed to the advancement of design. DIRTT has been persuading enough companies to think differently about interior space to grow to more than seven hundred employees (who call themselves DIRTTbags), with a list of clients that includes

Google. DIRTT wants to change what Jenkins calls the "tremendous loss with waste" in the initial construction of conventional spaces, and the follow-on waste created by renovations, with a cradle-to-grave view of sustainable best practices.

None of DIRTT's success would be possible if the value proposition was limited to arguing for reduced landfill tonnages and carbon emissions and offering a demonstrably competitive price tag. "We offer high-end design that is customized and beautiful," says Jenkins. "People don't want to sustain ugly."

●　　●　　●

"Sustainability" too often is seen as a corporate luxury, a feel-good option located well beyond the business plan and a company's set of core competencies and, as such, an issue with no bearing on priorities like productivity, competitiveness, innovation, and profitability. Canada's Best Managed Companies, however, are beginning to recognize the essential role of sustainability in their operations.

In recent polling, 71 percent of senior executives agreed that controlling cost, increasing efficiency, and reducing waste by adopting environmentally sound business practices was a high priority. Reducing the environmental impact of the company's business activities was cited by 61 percent, improving corporate social responsibility by 59 percent, demonstrating leadership on environmental issues by 56 percent, and influencing the public on business and environmental issues by 44 percent.

For many companies, sustainability is the "new normal" of business practices. They have been working ahead of the regulatory curve foremost in reducing energy consumption, waste, and their carbon footprints. They have also been looking for similar commitments in companies with which they partner or ally, which has a knock-on effect of spreading the priority of sustainability through market forces. Companies may find their opportunities increasingly limited in a business climate in which sustainability expectations have reached beyond activist consumers to enterprises in general.

Sustainability lies at a convergence of environmental, social, and economic considerations. Environmental considerations are the primary drivers. While "sustainability" means many things to many industries and their customers, it fundamentally means to "do no harm," or at least to "do less harm" while taking steps to eliminate that harm. To be truly heralded as environmentally "sustainable," best practices generally have to go beyond what the law or industry norms require. The social consideration is expressed by the effect best practices have on customer relations, employee satisfaction, the company's vision of its role in society, and the aspirations company executives themselves have for bettering society.

From the economic perspective, sustainability can be considered an adjunct of productivity, in which measurable waste is driven out of processes. Companies are recognizing that sustainable practices realize tangible financial benefits. We're seeing an increasing appreciation of the net benefits of "green IT," for example. Because a significant portion of global carbon dioxide emissions is directly attributed to information and communications technologies, IT has a key role to play in reducing energy consumption. The U.S. Environmental Protection Agency further estimates that about 60 percent of all disposed electronic goods are IT-related. Where sustainable practices themselves are not equally expensive as, or less expensive than, non-sustainable ones, they achieve gains that can in fact be measured because of net benefits in the sphere of social considerations, which can be expressed by customer loyalty and brand reputation.

Sustainable practices are becoming a hallmark of Best Managed Companies. Steam Whistle Brewing, which we discussed in Chapter 1, "Strategy: Brewing Up a Winning Formula for Marketplace Success," has one of the most all-inclusive corporate commitments to environmentally friendly practices. It uses refillable bottles with 30 percent more glass than normal, which makes them less prone to breakage and longer lasting (up to three times as long as a standard bottle), thus reducing waste and energy lost through recycling. It also paints the label on the bottle, so that in addition to trees not being pulped for paper labels, glue and dyes can't contaminate the water drained from the company's bottle washer. Every element of its packaging is recyclable, down to the bottle caps.

Steam Whistle partnered with Bullfrog Power in 2007 with a goal to power its Roundhouse brewery in Toronto with zero carbon emissions, drawing electricity only from wind farms and low-impact hydro generation. Rather than use conventional air conditioning at the brewery, it employs Enwave Deep-Water Cooling from Lake Ontario and saves on its electricity bill in the process. Heating is provided by steam from Enwave, which Steam Whistle draws on as required (and naturally uses it to power its signature steam whistle at the end of the working day). Its delivery trucks run on bio fuel containing soya and recycled restaurant oil. Its eye-catching Retro Electro vehicle is recharged by Bullfrog Power as well. Steam Whistle earned an Environmental Award of Excellence from the City of Toronto in 2009 for its use of alternative energy sources as well as its reduced energy consumption. It was also the winner in the Large Business category in the Ontario Ministry of the Environment's 2011 Minister's Award for Environmental Excellence.

The Retro Electro vehicle is exemplary of Steam Whistle's entrepreneurial verve and consistent ability to align genuine sustainable innovations with its brand. It began with a providential rehiring. "One of our former employees called us up and said he was tired of being a medical researcher in Seattle and wanted to become a beer rep," recalls brewery co-founder Greg Taylor of Retro Electro's innovator, Mike Kiraly. "We thought this guy was amazing. He'd worked with us for eight years while he got his PhD. We had talked about moving into the Vancouver market, but only when the time was right. So we said to Mike, 'Sure, move to BC.'"

"He loved vintage vehicles and had rebuilt an MG," adds Sybil Taylor, Greg Taylor's wife, who oversees communications for Steam Whistle. "He knew we had a green ethos, and he approached us a year into selling beer for us out west." Kiraly told them that he didn't have the advantage of the Roundhouse brewery in Toronto to physically anchor the brand in the minds and experience of local consumers. He wanted to have a delivery vehicle that truly stood out—something fun, fast, and green, both in brand-true livery and values. The company liked his idea and the result was the Retro Electro, a customized, all-electric 1958 Chevrolet Apache truck that Kiraly created and drives.

"We spent twice the money and time on the Retro Electro as we thought we would, but it was worth it," says Sybil Taylor. "The green vehicle out west became the embodiment of our brand. People all over the world started picking up on our story, sharing 'How people in Vancouver get their sustainable beer delivered to them, emissions free.'"

Cactus Club Cafe, which we discussed in Chapter 7, "Innovation: How Trendsetting Companies Embrace a Culture of Change," has been a pioneer in bringing sustainability principles to the menus of a chain restaurant. CEO Richard Jaffray and his restaurant chain espouse the philosophy of the "local food" movement, sourcing ingredients as close to the restaurant chain as possible. The chain is supplied by Vancouver's artisanal bakery

Terra Breads, for example, and secures seasonal vegetables from Winset Farms in Abbotsford. Poultry comes from the Fraser Valley.

There's far more to Cactus Club's commitment to socially and environmentally responsible sourcing than token, feel-good gestures. "One of the reasons other restaurant groups don't do it is that it's a lot of work," says Jaffray. "It's a challenge in sourcing local, fresh ingredients to get a large enough supply." Rather than saying the existing supplies are inadequate to its multiple-unit needs, Cactus Club has rolled up its sleeves to make the supply chain possible for locally sourced ingredients. It worked with West Coast Fishculture to create a market for steelhead salmon raised in Lois Lake. Jaffray says this freshwater aquaculture operation is protecting British Columbia's wild salmon stocks by not practising cage aquaculture in saltwater sites.

Cactus Club helped West Coast Fishculture to get its operation endorsed by the Vancouver Aquarium's Ocean Wise sustainable seafood program, of which Cactus Club was a founding member. The Lois Lake aquaculture site also conforms to the United Nations Food and Agriculture Organization's Code of Conduct for Responsible Fisheries. Working with Cactus Club to bring environmentally friendly product to market has benefited such suppliers well beyond the sales to the restaurant chain. "We can get suppliers access to a distribution network they wouldn't get on their own," says Jaffray. West Coast Fishculture's steelhead, for example, is now distributed by Sea Agra Seafood Ltd. and is available at the big-box retailer Costco.

It's on the other side of the country, in Atlantic Canada, that we encounter a Best Managed Companies winner working to tap the ocean's resources in a way that is sustainable in its harvesting while reducing its environmental impact as much as possible in its processing.

• • •

Acadian Seaplants has deep roots in Atlantic Canada's seaweed industry. As a boy in the community of Salmon River, Nova Scotia, Louis Deveau would watch his father spread what the Acadians of Baie Ste-Marie call *goémon de roche* (rockweed) on his garden as a fertilizer. After earning an engineering degree in 1957, Louis Deveau began a six-year stint in 1961 with what is now Fisheries and Oceans Canada, developing the snow crab and shrimp industries. From 1967 to 1979, he was employed by Marine Colloids of Rockland, Maine, travelling the world to source seaweed for processing into a food gum, carrageenan, and developing the seaweed industry in locations as far-flung as the Philippines and Indonesia. He also served as president of Marine Colloids' Canadian division, which he acquired in 1980. On that foundation, Deveau launched Acadian Seaplants, headquartered in Dartmouth, Nova Scotia, the following year.

In Atlantic Canada, the subsequent collapse of the groundfish fishery cast a pall over the economy and the lives of thousands who depended on it, directly or indirectly. Annual catches of close to 2 million tonnes in the mid-1960s fell to about 110,000 tonnes in the early 1990s. For shocked and chastened fisheries managers, concerns turned to the harvesting of seaweed, a resource many considered to be as inexhaustible as cod once was.

Rockweed is the most important commercial seaweed in Atlantic Canada. It grows abundantly in intertidal zones from the Arctic Circle to the New Jersey coast. Depending on the location, it produces anywhere from 20 to 45 percent new biomass every year. But the plant is no aquatic "weed"—it takes about two to five years for rockweed to develop fertile plants, and relative to other seaweeds, it has what are called "poor recruitment levels." The fact that it dominates the intertidal zone is believed to be the result of long-term succession from existing beds. If it is ever seriously over-harvested, it may have a difficult time re-establishing itself.

Rockweed has long been gathered by local people and used as plant fertilizer, but commercial exploitation of sea plants in Nova Scotia only began in the late 1950s. The red algae, Irish moss, found use as raw material for sodium alginate, a kind of gum used in everything from drink thickeners to water- and fire-proofing fabrics, and rockweed was harvested for "kelp meal," an organic fertilizer. Rockweed is still used today as a crop bio-stimulant and a plant growth regulator, but also to a substantial degree as an animal feed supplement, among a multitude of other food-chain applications.

When commercial harvesting of rockweed arrived, the province of Nova Scotia introduced a few exclusive-purchasing licences in its southwestern intertidal zones, but the vast majority of the resource in the province was open to unlimited harvest. Beginning in the mid-1980s, quotas were introduced in some areas, but the harvest regulation was haphazard. Even today in Nova Scotia, while harvesting in some places is controlled by provincial leases, a lease is not required by individuals gathering rockweed for personal use, and they can even do so in a leased area.

Rockweed is most plentiful in southwestern Nova Scotia and New Brunswick, at the entrance to the Bay of Fundy. Until the mid-1990s, there had been no rockweed harvesting to speak of in New Brunswick. The province opened its waters for the first time in 1995 to a commercial harvest through a memorandum of understanding between the provincial department of fishery and aquaculture and Fisheries and Oceans Canada. A three-year pilot project was launched, with a harvest quota of 10,000 tonnes.

Interested companies, individuals, and associations were asked to submit a harvest proposal to the Rockweed Management Committee (RMC). They were to show how they would achieve stated objectives in maximum employment, sustainability of the harvest, sound business principles, and environmental acceptability. After reviewing all of the proposals, the Rockweed Management Committee recommended that just one company, Acadian Seaplants, be awarded an exclusive licence to all three designated harvesting areas. It was the only proponent that was able to meet the RMC's criteria.

"We wanted to come in with a fresh approach and in a sustainable way," says Jean-Paul Deveau, who in 1986 joined the company founded by his father Louis and became its president in 1992. "We put a lot of work into our scientific resource management model to ensure that what we were doing would be sustainable forever."

When the Rockweed Management Committee for the New Brunswick pilot project requested harvest proposals, Acadian Seaplants used aerial photography and on-site verification of species type and depth. "We knew the exact amount of seaweed available," says Jean-Paul Deveau. "One of our researchers, a PhD, determined how much would grow, and we planned a harvest for every bed. We knew we could take 17 to 25 percent of the existing biomass annually because it grew there at 40 to 45 percent a year. We have far exceeded the requirements of the licences."

Acadian Seaplants employs an experienced team of seaweed resource managers as well as a world-renowned marine biologist, Dr. Raul Ugarte, to apply exacting, comprehensive, and technically sound marine plant management procedures and controls involving all of the company's harvesting territories. Acadian Seaplants also supports government licensing of harvesting territories to ensure industry accountability and the sustainability of the resource and its ecosystem.

Through five Atlantic Canadian processing facilities, the company turns seaweed in Nova Scotia, New Brunswick, and Prince Edward Island into innovative products for the global food and food-chain sectors. (It also operates a seasonal harvest in Maine out of an office in Pembroke.) Its products are sold to food, brewery, health, nutriceutical, cosmetic, animal feeds, and plant growth regulator markets in over seventy countries.

Acadian Seaplants also has a longstanding commitment to research in aquaculture as well as sustainable harvesting of wild seaweeds. In 2008, the company shared a Synergy Award for Innovation from the Natural Sciences and Engineering Research Council of Canada (NSERC) for its participation with scientists from the University of New Brunswick and Fisheries and Oceans Canada in research into integrated multi-trophic aquaculture (IMTA) research in the Bay of Fundy. "IMTA is rooted in an age-old, common-sense, recycling and farming practice in which the by-products from one species become nutritional inputs for another," the NSERC explained in announcing the award. The team had shown how nutrients released from salmon pens operated by team member Cooke Aquaculture were captured and used as food and energy by mussels and seaweeds, providing additional crops that were free from contaminants and of extremely high quality. In 2009, Canada's National Research Council recognized Acadian Seaplants as an Innovation Leader.

Acadian Seaplants' commitment to sustainability extends to processing of seaweed, which is harvested manually. "We could dry it mechanically using carbon fuel," says Jean-Paul Deveau. "Instead, we bought all or part of two old airports and dry the seaweed using the sun. It's like making hay every day for five months." This solar solution has reduced the amount of carbon fuels in drying from 80 percent of the energy needed to about 18 percent, saving about

5000 tonnes annually in greenhouse gas emissions. The company is also now exploring ways to turn the waste stream from processing into a value-added product.

Acadian Seaplants is known today as the leading seaweed research company in the world. That research has extended well beyond how seaweed can be exploited to ensuring that a maritime resource considered bounteous to the point of inexhaustible in fact remains that way for generations to come.

●　●　●

When Guelph, Ontario, closed its troubled organic-waste plant in 2006 and began shipping waste instead to an incinerator in Niagara Falls, New York, for processing, its citizens made it known that they wanted an at-home solution as part of the city's goal of becoming the greenest community in Canada. The old plant had been plagued by low waste conversion rates and odours. Trucking waste to an American incinerator would only contribute further to greenhouse gas emissions. In a 2008 survey, 68 percent of Guelph residents said they wanted the city to exceed the provincial waste diversion goal of 60 percent. The city set goals of 55 percent by 2011, 65 percent by 2016, and 70 percent by 2021. It needed a solution other than energy-from-waste, which the province does not recognize as a diversion strategy.

Any community serious about diverting waste from landfills needs to deal with organic matter, as it typically represents 40 percent of household waste by weight, with recyclable materials another 40 percent. Organic diversion also has significant benefits in job creation and the production of marketable material: composted topsoil that can be used by city parks departments and sold to land-scapers, gardeners, farmers, and the like. And so a new Organic

Waste Processing Facility was put out to tender, one that would stop the trucks from carrying organic matter across the border and allow Guelph to improve its waste diversion rate by 10 percent.

Maple Reinders of Mississauga, Ontario, got the nod for the $32.8 million project using a proven aerobic technology from the Netherlands. The facility employs sealable concrete tunnels, aerated floors, sprinkler systems, and a climate-control system to maximize the decomposition process; biofilter scrubbers from a Guelph company, BIOREM, control odours that could emanate from the plant.

Officially opened in September 2011, Guelph's plant can process 30,000 tonnes of "source-separated organics" per year. That is triple Guelph's current requirements, but the city is able to service nearby Kitchener-Waterloo as well and can accommodate future growth with the excess capacity.

In addition to serving as the general contractor on the new plant, Maple Reinders' AIM Environmental Group division is contracted to operate it and market the compost through a subsidiary, Wellington Organix. AIM has become one of Canada's leading enterprises in composting technology solutions, demolition, and soil remediation. With AIM, Maple Reinders has built a dozen such organic waste plants in Canada, including a major installation in Hamilton, Ontario. As with the Guelph operation, AIM manages the Hamilton Central Composting Facility, which takes in organic feedstock from household green-bin programs in Halton Region, Simcoe County, and Waterloo Region, as well as Haldimand County's leaf and yard program.

It's a high-tech approach to producing what otherwise would seem to be a low-tech product: fungible topsoil. The organic feedstock brought to the Hamilton facility goes through an extensive preparation and testing before it is turned into finished compost.

This includes a detailed testing program, a pasteurization cycle that kills all weed seeds and pathogens, and an advanced screening process. The result is the highest grade of unrestricted-use compost. "We turn waste into topsoil in fifty to sixty days," says Mike Reinders, president and COO of Maple Reinders, "and we sell it to farmers and landscapers."

Founded in 1967, the family-owned Maple Reinders calls itself the "Civil Environmental contractor of choice in Canada." In addition to its organic waste facilities, it designs and builds water and wastewater treatment facilities, energy-from-waste plants, and wind and solar power installations. As a general contractor, Maple Reinders is known for delivering green efficiencies. "We're building a couple new office buildings out west," Reinders notes. "We're employing better insulation, with high-efficiency heating and cooling" as well as passive energy-efficiency features like a white roof.

The Trisan Centre in Schomberg, Ontario, a multi-use recreational facility that includes a two-bay paramedic response station, incorporated such sustainable-design features as landscaping that reduces water requirements by half, rainwater capture for toilet flushing that reduces potable water use in the wastewater stream by half, and a roof design that reduces cooling needs in hot weather. The chair of the facility's arena praised the effort by Maple Reinders in bringing the project in on time and under budget when it opened in June 2009: "It's an amazing facility. These guys were amazing to work with." In August 2011, Maple Reinders secured the contract for the new RCMP facility in Prince George, BC, that would feature a solar air-heating wall, a solar hot-water system, improved exterior envelope insulation, and maximization of natural lighting.

The company is striving to reduce the environmental impact of its own activities. "We try to recycle as much as possible on job sites," says Mike Reinders. "We hire students for the summer to pull together as much scrap as they can, to take them to recycle sites. We have bins for steel, wood, and copper."

In its own company offices, Reinders says, "We're trying to capture all of our organic waste." Kitchen and cafeteria areas have green bins; battery bins divert mercury and other harmful metals from the municipal waste stream. The vice-president in charge of environmental matters makes a point of having no wastebasket in his office.

"We promote and advocate our employees becoming involved in different environmental activities," says Reinders. They participate in community events such as Earth Day cleanups. More broadly, Maple Reinders donates 10 percent of pre-tax earnings to charitable causes. Its support ranges from soup kitchens to Third World water projects to staff trips to build orphanages in Guatemala and Zambia. The company views these activities as an important aspect of personal growth and fulfillment, and not surprisingly, Maple Reinders has been heralded as one of the best small- to medium-sized Canadian companies to work for.

Providing others with sustainable solutions is not enough, summarizes Mike Reinders. "We want to practise what we preach."

●　　●　　●

"Practise what we preach," is a motto that applies well to DIRTT's efforts to change the way companies think about space and waste. A key component of DIRTT's eco-friendly interiors solution is its embrace of localized or distributed manufacturing. Not hauling wall components long distances on trucks (or across oceans on ships) reduces greenhouse gas emissions. But green is also good when measured by the bottom-line results of improved productivity. "If you have smaller footprints close to your clients," says president Scott Jenkins, "then you reduce significantly transportation costs and times, which improves exponentially our responsiveness. Time is money, and we want to be able to compress the construction cycle."

DIRTT achieves distributed manufacturing through its proprietary software design solution, ICE. It's part design tool, part video game, which allows clients to specify and visualize their interior design. "ICE software saves us people, which are the number-one over-budget issue, and allows us to manage highly efficient local facilities as if they were one plant," says Jenkins. "It's the backbone that allows the distributed manufacturing model to exist."

An associated software tool, ICEberg, is crucial to persuading clients of the value proposition of a manufactured interior. Its database allows clients to compare the quoted cost of a DIRTT interior to the construction costs of a conventional interior space in any North American location.

"We're doing things with highly skilled team members," says Jenkins, "and it's a challenge for us to show that our solutions are cost-competitive right out of the gate and are cost-compelling over their life cycle. If we're not cost-competitive out of the gate, we don't get to the second conversation. We have to prove the value proposition in the first conversation to get to the second one. And nine out of ten times, we're finding we're successful."

Jenkins says DIRTT has "a different thought process in a conventional construction environment." Conventional construction entails erecting walls with studs and drywall; wiring for power and data networks is hand placed. The initial construction of such interior spaces creates waste in cut materials. Then there is more waste when interiors have to change to accommodate different needs of an owner or a tenant. Walls, wiring, and flooring are torn out and the process starts all over again. DIRTT has been asking: "Why can't spaces be more flexible?" DIRTT provides a modular and adaptable kit of parts that can be moved, reused, and repurposed: robust walls, flooring and millwork, and reusable plug-and-play power and data systems.

DIRTT has also been showing clients how its flexible, manufactured modular solutions can be more efficient in the use of interior space. Simply replacing a swing door with a sliding one saves nine square feet in a typical office. DIRTT says it can reduce a ten-by-fifteen-foot office workspace to ten-by-ten without any sacrifice to the user. More efficient workspaces means less space overall, and less space overall means lower total construction costs, rental charges, and environmentally challenged overheads like heating and cooling. And because DIRTT's components are fabricated in an efficient, distributed-manufacturing facility, the company says its method eliminates the carbon-footprint comings and goings of a construction crew completing the same interior in a conventional manner.

DIRTT creates beautiful as well as efficient and environmentally friendly interiors that last. Its composite wall panels use non-toxic, water-based glues. You can order walls in the Breathe line that incorporate plants to scrub an interior's air for you. In DIRTT's view, "sustainability" comes down to the root "sustain," or to endure. In its interior design and construction niche, it wants to shift thinking away from waste reduction through recycling toward waste reduction through building things that are not expendable, because they are superbly engineered as well as adaptable, with less demand on the environment all through a product's life cycle.

Jenkins compares the DIRTT solution to a reusable water bottle versus one that can be recycled. "If you get to the third 'R' in 'reduce, reuse, recycle,' fundamentally you've failed," he says. As the company states: "Recycling happens when you've run out of ideas. Recycling shouldn't be your first thought—it should be your last."

The market has been listening. "We've almost doubled business in the last three years," says Jenkins. "We're almost at the tipping point of a lot of people saying, 'Wait a minute, this makes way more sense.' In downtowns, companies have bought into the flexibility. A functional space that's pleasing to a team member doesn't have to be as large as a conventional interior. We're creating a new bar that people have to aim for in manufactured quality. Europe and Asia already understand that manufactured is better in interior space. I think the paradigm is shifting in North America."

●  ●  ●

For many companies that are embracing sustainability, a "green" ethos is good business because consumers respond positively to it. These companies know that being sustainable in their practices also means talking about it. For privately held companies, bringing forward their sustainability virtues to customers—be they consumers or other businesses—can require initiative, as they may not be accustomed to the media liaison role that goes along with the mandatory reportage of a public company. All companies must learn how to draw attention to these best practices without being self-congratulatory. They must also recognize that anything less than a genuine commitment to sustainability will fail to sway opinion in a marketplace that has become inured to token practices. It's not enough anymore simply to recycle scrap office paper, much less to boast about it.

At Steam Whistle, the Electro Retro vehicle at once captures the company's genuine commitment to sustainability while embodying brand values, a powerful combination of best-practice and promotion. The company is savvy enough to have spread the positive message of the Electro Retro far beyond Vancouver, with a multi-episode video story prominently featured on its website. The locally sourced vegetables and eco-friendly farmed salmon on the dinner plates at Cactus Club similarly exemplify the restaurant chain's commitment to sustainable practices while engaging the customer directly with product that satisfies their own desires (and appetites) for a greener world.

Sustainability to DIRTT's Scott Jenkins is a strategic response that benefits businesses as well as the general economy. "In a volatile economy, companies largely will be successful and sustainable through technology," he argues. "And companies with sustainable solutions that deliver them with sustainable practices are huge generators of jobs."

# ATTRACTING AND RETAINING TALENT: BUILDING THE LATTICE

The Great Little Box Company is now a great deal more than boxes, which was all that the business was making in 1982 when Robert Meggy retrieved it from receivership. Meggy was thirty-six then, a certified management accountant who had served as a controller for a number of private companies. "Some of them were terribly run by families. I thought: 'Man, I can do better.'" Having visited the distressed corrugated box maker before the severe recession of the early 1980s hit, Meggy had seen phones ringing and left unanswered. It made him think there was potential in the operation. Because the name "Great Little Box Company" was already in the Yellow Pages, he decided to keep it.

The company had just two employees, a machine operator and a salesperson, and he promptly hired a third, a new immigrant from Vietnam. That third hiring is still with the Great Little Box Company and has been joined by 250 others. Today it's the only company in Canada to manufacture corrugated boxes, folding cartons, labels, and foam packaging under one roof. Above and beyond its continued success and growth as an enterprise, the Great Little Box Company has become widely recognized as one of

Canada's most desirable employers. In 2011, it was named for the eighth consecutive year one of the top one hundred companies to work for. Employee turnover, says Meggy, "is almost zero."

In the course of evaluating the Canada's Best Managed Companies applicants, Deloitte met with more than 350 CEOs across the country like Robert Meggy. Attracting and retaining talent emerged as a substantial issue in our conversation. We've seen a corresponding acceleration among Best Managed Companies in the areas of creating and executing strategies for talent acquisition and retention, as well as in related transition and succession activities.

It's not enough for a company to strive to retain as much talent as possible. Plans that simply attempt to make employees captive through benefit packages, for example, can make the company itself a captive of its static workforce. The goal is to make each company a place that motivated talent wants to help grow and prosper, not a place that it doesn't want to leave. Companies need to have a plan to attract, retain, and engage *top performers*. Such a plan also helps to create those performers.

All enterprises grapple with the challenges of attracting and selecting new talent and of keeping that talent within the organization. The value of human capital is often intangible, but the costs of neglecting it are not. Companies with high turnover rates have correspondingly high costs of finding and replacing their workforce.

If a company is unable to retain its talent, succession planning in leadership is compromised. Indeed, as we saw in Chapter 2, "Leadership: Inverting the Pyramid to Empower the Workforce," many organizations are inverting the standard pyramid of leadership and empowering the broad base of the organization. If that base is not properly recruited and supported, leadership by and from within the workplace can neither function nor emerge. Effective management ensures that the organization evolves fluidly, so that talent gaps don't appear because succession planning in leadership roles has been ignored.

Companies that fail to hire well and train and retain good employees are also sacrificing considerable opportunities for innovation. Great companies testify to the importance of their employees in bringing forward ideas that improve products and processes. They are also becoming increasingly aware of the importance of workplace diversity in tapping internal intelligence to understand marketplace opportunities, both domestically and globally.

Employees of highly rated companies look forward to coming to work, and they drive improvement and change throughout an organization. Most important perhaps, these employees carry their enthusiasm into their relationships with customers and strategic allies. Conversely, unmotivated and dissatisfied employees project those sentiments into the marketplace as the persona of their company.

A theme we constantly encounter in examples of great employers is *engagement*. It wasn't so long ago that people routinely worked for one employer for an entire career: Job loyalty was a given. Today, the *best* employees need to have good reasons to stay, but many organizations fail to provide them. If organizations want to hang on to their highest performers and develop future leaders, they need to understand what their people want, both personally and professionally. In addition to encouraging retention of the best and brightest talent, higher employee engagement fosters a culture that motivates people to perform to their full potential.

In this chapter we meet four of Canada's Best Managed Companies that have faced unique challenges in attracting and retaining workplace talent, and have applied their own solutions to great effect.

● ● ●

Cultivating fresh talent at Robert Meggy's company comes down to not *how* you attract it but *who* you attract. There is a rigorous methodology to the Great Little Box Company's hiring practices. The company is so well known as a great place to work, and has such low turnover, that it can afford to be extremely judicious in its screening of potential new employees.

"Most companies interview candidates twice," says Meggy. "We do seven or eight interviews with anyone we hire, and we include the people they would be working with in the interview process. We want to hire the right people and make sure they stay."

Hirings that don't work out are a drain on any organization. If they're a poor fit, they can negatively impact productivity and morale and may have to be terminated. If they're a good fit and decide to find work elsewhere, they take with them experience, knowledge, and a big investment in training costs. Few companies can really afford to churn through employees. The vast majority would like to find them and keep them, and only lose them for reasons largely beyond their control. Precious few companies have the Great Little Box Company's track record for hiring well and keeping people on the payroll.

Meggy long ago learned that socializing is a key differentiator between the hirings that stay with the company and the ones that leave. "You spend most of your waking hours with people you work with," he says. It followed that people who spend that much time with each other should get along, and if the company could provide people who appear to be a good fit with the means to socialize and interact, they would be more committed to each other and the workplace. "We try to hire people who are interested in company social events. We've found that with people who do not go to social events, 75 percent are not going to be there in a year."

This is not to say that Meggy's only solution to attracting and retaining talent is throwing plenty of social events. Rather, his company has paid close attention to the issue of work–life balance and has determined where the workplace can fulfill social needs. The result is a broad basket of compensations, many of them focused on making it possible for people to live longer, healthier lives.

Fresh fruit is made available every day, at no charge. After Christmas holidays, the company holds a body mass index (BMI) contest to help employees shed extra weight. It has paid employees to quit smoking. There's a fitness centre with a personal trainer, open twenty-four hours, seven days a week, and employees can bring a friend on weekends. The company bought land fronting on the Fraser River and created a company park that includes beach volleyball. Employees have their own vegetable gardens. They take part in paintball and golf tournaments and 10K runs together.

Yet there's more to the company's approach than seeming perks. "People are the biggest asset you have," Meggy advises. "We want to make sure people stay. We look a lot at needs and wants." And while a free fitness centre and vegetable gardens are appreciated, what employees need and want above all is effective communication. They want to know how they and the company are doing; they also want to be able to say what they and the company should be doing. And they want to be rewarded—not only monetarily or through benefits, but through a sense of being valued and having a future in the organization, along with recognition for a job well done.

Open and effective communication is one of the key factors in managing talent. A company should provide a regular forum for open communication and collaboration. "People generally want to know what's going on," says Meggy, with their own careers and with the company. Knowing what's going on in both cases creates trust and loyalty, and employees who feel genuinely engaged create a more profitable company that can afford the perks like the waterfront park and the fitness centre.

Meggy creates trust with employees by running the company "open book." Every month, all employees are shown a consolidated statement of earnings and a balance sheet along with stated goals and objectives from different departments so they have a complete understanding of the current situation and the direction of the company. Employees have good reason to want to know how the company is performing. Profitability makes possible the array of benefits employees enjoy, including education bursaries for their children. Fifteen percent of earnings is distributed among all employees in a profit-sharing plan that makes no distinctions according to seniority, income level, or hierarchy. Everybody, whether they're in the office or plant, gets the same share. The company has a small arsenal of discretionary remunerations in addition to profit sharing. It pays for suggestions that improve operations, anywhere from $10 to $1000, depending on the results. Employees nominate each other for special recognition, and rewards range from gift certificates to a special parking spot (the company otherwise has no designated parking spots for management).

The company consults with employees and departments in creating a three-year sales plan—the latest plan is called the Big Outrageous eXtravanganza (Box) Goal. Annual business planning is done in five strategic planning meetings, each of them involving a different cross-section of the company with no more than a dozen people involved from all levels of the organization to provide focus. The meeting themes are Sales Increase, Cost Reduction, How to Improve Customer Service, Employee Wellness, and SWOT (Strengths, Weaknesses, Opportunities and Threats). It also sets an annual "stretch goal" for profitability, and if it's met, the company celebrates by taking the staff on a free vacation. With sales up 17 percent and the company achieving record profits in 2011, the employees were rewarded with a trip to Puerto Vallarta, Mexico. The entire company went to the resort in two five-day overlapping getaways.

Top-performing companies need to regularly review their compensation and benefit structure to ensure it meets the needs of its employees and compares favourably with marketplace standards. One useful insight in this regard is that different generations of employees have particular priorities in compensation. Some place greater emphasis on career advancement than others; some are more interested in measurable compensation, or in work–life balance. To this end, we stress the importance of workforce analytics, which involves using statistical models that integrate internal and external data to predict future workforce and talent-related behaviour and events. These models help companies focus limited resources on critical talent decisions. They have been able to predict the probability of a particular employee leaving within six months and provide the most likely reasons.

Beyond wages, bonuses, and benefits, the Great Little Box Company compensates employees by giving them clear visibility in their career path. "I'm very strong on feedback," says Meggy. "Individuals set quarterly goals and review them with supervisors. They also have an annual meeting to address short-term and long-term goals." When asked what causes him to lose employees, Meggy can only offer two scenarios: Someone decides not to return from maternity leave, or an employee feels he or she does not have an opportunity for advancement opening up quickly enough and chooses to take a more senior position elsewhere. "If anyone quits here, we should know in advance. Leaving for the sake of leaving rarely happens."

●  ●  ●

If you want examples of attracting and retaining talent at Saskatchewan's Alliance Energy Group of Companies, look no further than its president, Bryan Leverick, and its CEO, Paul McLellan. Leverick has been with Alliance Energy for thirty-seven years, McLellan for thirty-five. They both started out at the company as electricians. They are also both third-generation electricians, and Leverick's son became one as well.

It's not unusual to find second- or third-generation employees. The Alliance Energy Group of Companies is composed of two firms, Alliance Energy Ltd., which was established in 1983, and Sun Electric (1975) Ltd., which dates back to 1913 and was reorganized in 1975. Sun Electric began with a store that opened in Regina only eight years after the province entered Confederation. While it long maintained a storefront operation, Sun Electric developed a reputation foremost as an electrical contractor, playing an important role in the provincial capital's development. Today Alliance Energy Group of Companies provides a full complement of services, making it one of the largest, most respected electrical contractors in Saskatchewan. Its Industrial/Commercial/Institutional Division provides services ranging from new systems design and installation to upgrades and expansions to trouble shooting, testing, and repair. Its Services Division provides budgeting, quotations, and electrical design-build services, while also offering service, preventative maintenance, and data/telecommunication cabling.

Paul McLellan's father was an electrician at Alliance Energy, and like a lot of kids whose dads were electricians, McLellan found summer work as a teen in the trade. He went away to university and earned a bachelor's degree, thought about medicine, and then came back to Alliance Energy to work. He decided if he wanted to be serious about the business he should do the full apprenticeship and earn his licence. Many years later, at age fifty, he earned an MBA, and the combination of licensed electrician as his trade and a master's degree in business administration as his highest level of education sometimes gives pause.

"The electrical trade has been extremely favourable for young people," says Leverick. "We get lots and lots of nineteen- to twenty-year-olds applying for apprenticeships, and we have an elaborate apprenticeship system in Saskatchewan." One of the appeals of the electrician's trade is that the skill is both portable and in demand. Apprenticeship systems vary across the country, but journeymen can work anywhere once licensed. And in Saskatchewan, where an energy boom saw the province sidestep the 2008–09 recession, electricians are no longer in a seasonal trade. "The old thinking of an electrician working six to eight months per year doesn't apply," says Leverick. "The economy also has allowed us to increase wages. We haven't had a layoff in Saskatoon since 1994." At the Saskatchewan Institute of Applied Science and Technology, which is the main provider of trades training in the province, electrical is the largest of all the apprenticed trades.

Maintaining a talent pipeline is a critical human-resources objective. While the problem of securing an adequate supply of talent varies widely according to industries and regions, in the wake of a recession we have seen that quality applicants are getting harder to find even as applications for most positions have remained high. Two converging trends are fuelling this talent shortage. First, as the economy recovers and new opportunities become available, employees who were hesitant to move during the downturn may begin to search for new jobs, leaving behind a talent gap. Second, as the workforce ages, many senior staff are approaching retirement. Companies that have not identified appropriate successors will be hardest hit by this loss of institutional knowledge.

Alliance Energy has helped meet its own demand for new employees by playing a leading role in the apprenticeship system, helping to create a highly desirable trade category for young people. "We've always given back to the industry," says McLellan. He spearheaded the creation of the Saskatchewan Apprenticeship and Trades Certification Commission (SATCC) and served as its chair for ten years before moving on in 2010. SATCC in turn contracts trades training to the Saskatchewan Institute of Applied Science and Technology. Adds Leverick: "We've always had at least one person from the company on the Saskatchewan Electrical Trade Advisory Board," which reports to SATCC. Two Alliance Energy employees currently are on that board, including Leverick, who has been a member of it for years.

Alliance Energy has long worked to develop its own licensed electricians by attracting the apprentices who need four full years of field work along with four levels of technical training of eight to nine weeks each. Alliance takes on about 120 new apprentices a year. "There's a huge scramble for trades people," says Leverick. "Co-op systems are the latest trend, but we've been doing it by training our own for a long time."

The designation as one of Canada's Best Managed Companies has helped to attract and retain talent. "It has increased the level of pride," says Leverick. "We're the only electrical contractor in the province to be recognized by the Best Managed program."

"We work hard to ensure our apprentices and trades people are the best," says McLellan. Alliance does that by giving these new workers variety. Alliance's work portfolio is such that it can offer something of everything—industrial, commercial, institutional, service, and residential work—so it sees a broad aspect of the trade. "A lot of people come to us saying they had the company recommended to them because of the variety of work."

That variety not only helps get them in the door, but also helps retain them. So does a corporate commitment to ongoing training for its employees. "We know there is a high cost to train people, but it's really expensive not to," says Leverick. "It's not just a philosophy, but a practice of Alliance Energy to promote ongoing training. The more people are trained, the better off the company is. Training opens peoples' minds. If you're open to training all the time, you're open to change and to acquiring new skill sets." The workplace is not only where you earn a paycheque, but also where you learn and grow. "Eighty percent of what people know has been learned on the job."

Retaining employees is a challenge in an industry that relies on trades people who are in broad demand and have highly portable skills and that also has become attuned to fulfilling pledges of workplace diversity. "Retaining people has been an issue," says Leverick. "We have trained literally thousands of apprentices. We do get poached. But we tend to lose them to customers like the mining sector, not to competitors in electrical contracting." Leverick himself, a former field electrician, is proof positive of one of the ways Alliance is able to hold on to valued employees: by giving them the opportunity to migrate out of the field if they choose and into the office. "About 10 percent of our staff are in the office," says Leverick. "The rest are in the field. Over half of our office staff has come from the field. That opportunity has been important to retention." This doesn't happen haphazardly. Alliance Energy confers with employees to map career paths. As workers try to map out their employment futures, Alliance Energy does its best to ensure that the map doesn't have to wander outside the opportunities it affords.

● ● ●

For some industries, the notion of zero turnover in employees, or of retaining highly skilled employees by offering different avenues of professional growth (as Alliance Energy has in moving field electricians into office roles), is an impossible dream. Such is the case in the grocery retail business, where the experiences and strategies of Farm Boy, a private chain in eastern Ontario, are instructive for businesses in any sector of the economy for which a large part of the workforce is part-time or is looking for employment that is strictly temporary. At the same time, the company has full-time staff who need to be found, retained, and promoted, all while overseeing a substantial workforce who may come to Farm Boy to work for a relatively short period in their lives but must often serve as the face of customer service.

"The turnover in the industry is 55 to 60 percent per year," says Gilles Groulx, Farm Boy's vice-president of human resources. "Everybody wants to be better, but it's the reality of the business, which has students working part-time and people going back to school." He estimates half of Farm Boy's 1400 employees are part-time. About a hundred employees work full-time at the company's home office; Farm Boy also operates a central facility for distribution and meat preparation, as well as a commissary that prepares items for its eleven stores, ten of which are around Ottawa, one of which is in Cornwall.

Farm Boy is a regional grocery store chain that is growing through distinctive product and retail strategies. Fulfilling its staffing needs has led Farm Boy to develop different strategies for different workforce categories. "Our best recruiting tool is our own website," says Groulx. A careers page provides a listing of every available position, with a link to a form to which a résumé can be attached and sent immediately to the human resources department. "An IT project manager or a payroll manager might be more difficult to find, and we may use a professional recruiting company. But that only occurs three or four times a year." Otherwise, Farm Boy has been successful using services like Workopolis for more professional positions that need to be filled.

All hirings move through three levels of assessment. Every store has a human resources assistant who prescreens candidates for any position there. Prescreened candidates then move on to a second-level interview with the manager of whatever department they will report to, with final interviews performed by the store manager. A similar three-tier process is followed for head-office jobs: prescreening by the human-resources assistant, followed by an interview by the specialist in the job field, and a final assessment by Groulx.

For full-time staff, Farm Boy provides a comprehensive compensation package. Department and store managers are entitled to quarterly bonuses. Benefits include dental and health care, short-term and long-term disability insurance, sick days, and a pension plan. It recently introduced group insurance for vehicles and homes. But one of the most successful benefits has been cheaper groceries. In 2011, all staff began receiving a 10 percent discount on their Farm Boy grocery bills. "It's helped us a lot and it's been very well received," says Groulx. For anyone raising a household of teenagers, lopping 10 percent off the monthly grocery bill is not a trivial benefit.

"There is constant training and coaching," Groulx says, through programs administered by a learning and development director at head office. Customer service standards are also assessed four times a year in every department. Training and evaluation measures individual performance as well as company-wide delivery on customer service. In 2011, it introduced an advanced service training program for meat department teams, which involves employee self-assessments and product knowledge retention, all with the goal of building engagement, team pride, and customer satisfaction.

"I promote from within every chance I get," Groulx adds. "We're looking for people who have a sense of urgency about getting things done. They show they know 'the Farm Boy way.'"

●　●　●

Brock Solutions of Kitchener, Ontario, is an engineering solutions company with an almost bewildering variety of projects to its name. It focuses on real-time operational solutions in manufacturing, heavy industries, and transportation and logistics, and the skills it has demonstrated globally have resulted in assignments ranging from tunnel boring to food processing to consumer products to airline baggage handling and passenger processing. Its SmartSuite, which employs software and tagged barcodes, is a module of products that provide comprehensive solutions for passenger and baggage handling at airports around the world.

"The bulk of our employees are highly educated people, in engineering, computer sciences, and other disciplines," says president and co-CEO Vivienne Ojala. "A lot of the appeal of working for Brock Solutions is the work itself. We have fun, challenging projects that attract people. That, together with a very 'flat' organization, makes us attractive as an employer. I know a lot of companies pay lip service to that idea, but we have no titles on our business cards."

Brock Solutions is a less-than-typical workplace in that it does not design and manufacture a particular product in assembly-line fashion. The company is very project-driven, and these projects demand solutions that go beyond software and machinery. As a professional services firm with an enviable reputation for making every project work and for delivering on time, it has the skill sets and proven approach to project management that make it attractive to clients with complicated challenges in the realm of real-time solutions engineering. Brock Solutions has excelled in finding ways to tackle such diverse projects from a human-resources perspective.

Brock Solutions is exemplary of two related trends in human resources: the "flat" organization and "lattice careers." Companies on average are about 25 percent less hierarchical than in industrial-age talent development models, and as we discussed in Chapter 2, "Leadership: Inverting the Pyramid to Empower the Workforce," employees in what were once the lower strata of a company's reporting chart are being empowered with decision-making and greater autonomy. As organizations have become flatter, the classic ladder model of upward promotion has been replaced by a lattice architecture, a term inspired by the mathematical concept of a lattice as a multidimensional structure that extends infinitely in any direction.

"I use the term 'network,'" says Ojala, "but 'lattice' is good as well." In a lattice-oriented workplace like Brock Solutions, employees move independent of formal hierarchies into different assignments and challenges, developing new skill sets along the way. Instead of a strict vertical model of increasing seniority, a lattice environment seeks to deliver growth for an employee with multidirectional movement. Employees can explore a multiplicity of options to build a career, redefining what "career progression" means. This workplace has also become more dynamic and virtual.

Technology is creating new possibilities for where, when, and how work gets done. Globalization, virtualization, modular job and process designs, and team-based project work have each accelerated the lattice trend. Employees can find this approach more personally fulfilling, and the enterprise increases the net intelligence and capability of its workforce, all while providing incentive for valued employees to remain with the organization.

"People take on projects and they are given the tools and responsibilities to fulfill their roles," says Ojala. "We're not about pay scales or hierarchy." On one project, an employee might be a technical lead, and on another, that person might be the project manager. "On each project, we try to marry the technical knowledge it requires from an employee with the needs of clients on the level of personal interaction." The composition of a given team thus might change, depending on the client and the project.

Brock Solutions offers what many employees yearn for: fresh challenges, variety in work experience, and the opportunity for growth through different team roles. Opportunity also comes relatively quickly. "It's not unusual for new grads coming out of university to be running a project for us on their own after two to five years. Or they become really capable technical leads with specialized knowledge."

People who come to work for Brock Solutions are immersed in a culture of teamwork with flexible, adaptable roles. "We're not so much about smart 'superstars' as we are about smart teams," says Ojala. "Our projects are too big for any single person. Instead, we put a lot of people together who want to work in a team environment. Collectively, we do some pretty impressive projects."

Among its recent achievements is its Smart Drop Baggage Image and Weight Identification System (BIWIS), which captures image and weight information for each bag checked into the system, and has been deployed at Toronto's Pearson International Airport and at Edmonton International Airport. It has also been working with Delta Airlines to upgrade their baggage systems, and was awarded by Delta two new baggage system projects in New York, at JFK International Airport's Terminal 4 international hub and LaGuardia Airport's domestic hub. In concert with Lockheed Martin, it has been taking the latest Explosive Detection System (EDS) technology and integrating it into live airport operations in order to evaluate performance criteria on behalf of the U.S. Transportation Security Administration.

Executing projects of the scale and sophistication that Brock Solutions typically manages requires an accommodating, supportive culture. Staff focused on completing a particular project need to be able to see beyond it where having a career at Brock Solutions is concerned. With projects often having to be completed in distant locations, employees also need an assignment to unfold as an enjoyable, stimulating challenge, not as an ordeal. "Our culture is important," says Ojala. "We try to have a flexible environment. Our work is for the real world, and it's driven by project life cycles. Someone might be in the office for a while, then travelling to deal with the project and the client. We expect people to be flexible, but we're flexible in return."

The company is not prescriptive in workflow management. Every project and every team is different, and the company allows teams to organize their own approach. This flexibility in part recognizes the changing face of work–life balance in the workplace in general. Three out of four married men now live in dual-career households, up from one in two in 1977. Work–life conflict for men as a result is far more prevalent, while women continue to juggle the needs of family and employer.

"Our teams come up with their own schedules," says Ojala.

"They might decide to be ten days on, four days off, for example, depending on the project. And we try to encourage teams to have fun. Work has to be fun. It can't be a chore to come here." The company encourages social events and supports sports teams. Brock Solutions employees play dodgeball and hockey and enter running events. The Vancouver office participates in the Vancouver Sun Run, Canada's largest 10K road race and the second-largest timed 10K in the world, and the company pays their entry fees.

Like the Great Little Box Company, Brock Solutions does not leave hiring to a strictly human-resources function. It engages employees in assessing candidates. Employees of similar age are brought in to interview new graduates, and with co-op students the company enlists employees one to two years out of such programs. An older employee, usually one with technical knowledge, will also be involved in the interview process. One element of hiring Ojala stresses is that the process is not just about a company deciding it likes a particular candidate. "It's more important that they want to work here. That's 70 percent of what's needed to make a hiring successful."

As Ojala's caution indicates, companies can focus too much on themselves. Instead of asking, "What do we want from this candidate?" they need to be paying closer attention to the candidate's expectations. Why do they even want to work here? Do they understand our culture? Are they a good fit for the approach we take? And while Ojala supports the idea of having existing employees involved in the hiring process, she cautions: "You have to be careful you don't end up with all the same kind of people." Employee vetting shouldn't be allowed to create a monoculture or a like-minded clique. "Our employees are from thirty different countries and they speak as many different languages," she says. "We're culturally and religiously diverse. Any kind of diversification you can name, we have it. And personally I think that's very important."

Workplace diversity delivers a variety of competitive advantages. No company does itself a favour by limiting its potential talent pool according to gender, culture, ethnicity, or nationality, especially when highly qualified candidates are in short supply. Companies are also recognizing that as their client base becomes more diverse, whether through changing domestic demographics or their globalization efforts, a workforce that reflects that diversity is to both their credit and benefit. Some of that benefit comes from the face that the company turns to its customer base. Companies have also found that a diverse workforce helps it better understand the needs and preferences of certain cultural communities. Where companies are operating globally, especially in emerging markets, it has become vital to hire locally and not simply send skilled workers or executives (with or without language skills) to run international divisions or offices. Talent exists in these markets, and companies need to tap it.

"We post jobs on the Web, and the reality of the Web is that it's an environment where people all around the world can apply," says Ojala. "As we work around the globe, we do look for people in those areas, or we partner with organizations that have feet on the ground." That said, the company has not had to go out of its way to recruit internationally. Brock Solutions has benefited from Canadian immigration policy in providing a strong pool of skilled candidates. "A lot of educated people are coming here from other countries. We're hiring new Canadians, people who have already decided to come here. We often find that they come to Canada and do a year of a master's degree, which helps them to integrate into the culture." Brock Solutions also provides new employees with English language training if required.

Ojala says the diversity of its employees has proved beneficial in some projects. For a recent contract in Brazil, the company happened to have a young Brazilian on staff and so assigned him to it. "We married his cultural knowledge with specific industry knowledge on the team." But Ojala stresses that Brock Solutions' workforce is not a collection of individual cultures. Its great strength, she says, is that it is autonomous and mutually supportive. It allows people of diverse cultural backgrounds to work together with common goals and interests, and insulates individuals from hostilities or discordance that may be present in project sites.

In Saskatchewan, the high demand among employers for skilled trades has helped to advance the cause of workplace diversity, and Alliance Energy has been at the forefront of this movement. The electrical trade is still an overwhelmingly male profession: Only 1 percent of licensed electricians in Saskatchewan are women, but rather remarkably, 15 percent of those women work for Alliance Energy. "The company is known as the one that trains women in the electrical trade in Saskatchewan," says Paul McLellan.

"We absolutely look for a diverse workforce," says McLellan. "Women bring a different perspective to the trade. We work in a lot of offices where women are the majority of employees, and they like seeing women in the trade." The physical demands of the trade aren't considered to present nearly the barriers to women as was once thought. A more pragmatic issue to overcome is that the Saskatchewan Institute of Applied Science and Technology's training locations for electricians, in Moose Jaw and Prince Albert, are relatively remote and can discourage women with children from entering into an apprenticeship.

Alliance Energy and the electrician trade in general in Saskatchewan have also made great strides in providing employment to Aboriginal people. The company has a working partnership, which includes apprenticeship training, with Tron Power Inc., a contractor with a long history in the mining industry that was acquired by English River First Nation in 1997. Promoting apprenticeship training among the province's Aboriginal peoples was a priority of McLellan during his leadership of SATCC. McLellan notes that, percentage-wise, Aboriginal participation in the electrical apprenticeship system is actually representative of the Aboriginal population of the province, which is not typical of trades training or almost any other profession, for that matter. "It's not something that's been built overnight," says Leverick, "but the results are wonderful."

Brock Solutions has a compensation model that Ojala says "supports a self-motivated and high-performing kind of individual. We're very much performance based." Like the Great Little Box Company, Brock Solutions uses profit-sharing. Ten percent of Brock Solutions' pre-tax profits are shared across the company. A portion is prorated to salary, with the rest tied to performance. There are also target bonuses for employees in leadership roles. It further offers profit-sharing through ownership, with up to 20 percent available for employees to have a minority interest. Alliance Energy has a bonus structure, which is based on meeting individual goals. The company is also owned by employees. While equity is limited to senior management, opportunities were expanded among Alliance management a few years ago. If extending the ownership opportunity to even more employees is called for, the company is prepared to do so.

Ojala says that Brock Solutions currently has a 3 to 5 percent turnover rate for employees it would have preferred not to lose. "You ideally want that at zero, but it's impractical to think you can ever achieve that. What do you do when someone gets married and their spouse gets a job elsewhere?"

The company's employee retention challenges derive from the project-oriented nature of the business. One issue is the life cycles of projects. Because these projects are geographically dispersed, at some point in the course of the project a team member usually has to travel. The opportunity to see the world is a great attraction for younger employees, but it can become harder for them to manage when they are married and raising children. "Our biggest challenge in retention is at the end of a project. People's minds start to wander, and they wonder what they're doing next. They're more open to doing something different at the end of a project than in the middle."

"We do try to be cognizant of the needs of a family," says Ojala. "A general rule is to treat people the way you want to be treated yourself. I know it's 'motherhood,' but it works." The company pays for individual YMCA memberships for employees, which makes it inexpensive for them to top up a membership category to "family." On some of its sports teams, spouses and partners participate. For the annual company meeting and staff party in Kitchener, Brock Solutions flies in everyone in with their spouses or guests, all expenses paid.

The companies discussed in this chapter have been able to manage their human capital in the best interests of themselves, their clients, and their employees. They have done so in part by optimizing the essential attraction of the work. Whatever it is that employees are being asked to do, they are engaged, challenged, and rewarded. In the case of Brock Solutions, Ojala notes that the company can't change the project-based nature of its business. "But we can make the work enjoyable," she says. For many employees, any company with a commitment to "enjoyment" is already a long way ahead in attracting and retaining top talent.

# 11

# PRODUCTIVITY: SCRAPPING THE TEMPLATE TO GET LEAN, NOT MEAN

You have probably heard the old carpenter's adage: "Measure twice, cut once." It's timeworn advice to double-check in order to eliminate error and reduce waste. But for Winnipeg's FLOFORM, the amount of measuring that went into producing one countertop was repetitive, redundant, time-consuming, and a source of error and waste in itself.

FLOFORM needed to get rid of cardboard—the cardboard being carried around by installers for making templates, which were then being gathered and driven around in trucks and being remeasured at one of its fabricating shops. Getting rid of cardboard promised tremendous savings in the production process, but doing away with cardboard, tape, and knives would also be expensive in terms of the required technology. FLOFORM, however, could see beyond that initial investment and recognized the array of benefits in changing one of its most basic processes. There was ultimately money to be saved, but there were also tremendous dividends in competitiveness, its relationship with customers, and the role and engagement of its workforce. FLOFORM thus ended up doing much more than getting rid of cardboard. It used the essential goal of improving productivity where production of a particular countertop is concerned as a means to improve its business on an array of other fronts.

The power of productivity to drive positive change is one of its least understood qualities, and this is not surprising, because productivity itself is often poorly understood. It is a fundamental issue not only for individual companies, but also for the Canadian economy and the standard of living we have come to enjoy and expect.

● ● ●

Productivity is a measure of efficiency in how goods and services are produced. At its core, it is fundamentally a human measure, which is why it is often referred to as *labour productivity*—a metric of the value that the average employed individual creates in each hour of work. Companies can employ other metrics to define aspects of productivity, but they remain inseparable from the human factor. Even with material waste, the underlying cause ultimately requires a human solution, whether it is better training, better workflow or other processes, or better technology with which to equip the worker.

In the past, a favourable exchange rate and a preferred access to U.S. markets through proximity and free trade served to insulate the Canadian economy and protect our standard of living. Those advantages have been eroding: The dollar has reached parity (and sometimes exceeds it), and the globalization of the economy has created much greater competition for Canada's manufacturers, both for export products and domestic consumption.

The Conference Board of Canada has called labour productivity, which measures how efficiently goods and services are produced, "the single most important determinant of a country's per capita income over the longer term. Countries that are innovative and able to adapt to the ebb and flow of the new global economy boast high productivity and thus a superior standard of living."

Canadian industry's essential problem of low productivity has been growing for some thirty years. Deloitte has identified six factors contributing to Canada's productivity gap. In addition to the historic sheltering of the Canadian economy—and doubtless arising from it—business leaders have been risk-averse, as groundbreaking polling by Deloitte in 2011 revealed. There has been inefficient and insufficient support for innovation. The economy has lacked risk capital for start-up companies that are wellsprings of innovation. Companies have chronically under-invested in machinery and equipment. Finally, changing demographics have created increasing competition for human capital: The departure of baby boomers from the labour pool has placed downward pressure on the number of Canadians in the workforce along with average working hours.

One of the most misunderstood aspects of productivity is the role of labour itself. Improving productivity does not mean that Canadians must work longer hours for less money. Instead, the Canadian economy must increase the number of people employed in high-paying jobs, producing premium outputs.

The Best Managed Companies winners discussed in this chapter have grappled with Canada's productivity challenges and found ways to innovate in their manufacturing processes and product offerings while confronting competition that has become increasingly global.

● ● ●

A cornerstone of many productivity initiatives is "lean" manufacturing. The concept's application varies widely among companies, but they share the goal of improving productivity by driving out waste. In the manufacturing process, waste can take many forms, but it is often related to time. The Toyota production system, with its "just in time" philosophy, is considered one of the main inspirations for today's lean strategies. Time can represent many different aspects of production where revenues are lost to inefficiency. Inventory is a popular target of lean regimens, as raw materials awaiting production and finished products that sit idle in a warehouse are great accumulators of a host of inefficiencies.

Lean manufacturing for FLOFORM has meant using technology to greatly simplify the process by reducing the number of steps, and with them opportunities for mistakes, along with the time to fulfill an order and a host of associated costs. It has also meant getting rid of a lot of cardboard.

Founded in 1961, FLOFORM of Winnipeg manufactures laminate, solid surface, natural stone, and quartz countertops for Western Canada and the Washington and Oregon markets. The acquisition of Fineline Pacific of Seattle doubled the company's size in 2008, and it is the only countertop manufacturer in Western Canada that manufactures all the products that it sells. FLOFORM sells through multiple channels: direct to consumers, through dealers like design professionals and cabinetmakers, and through retailers like Costco and the Home Depot. On the direct-to-consumer side, FLOFORM will install the counter for you or let you do it yourself. You can book a free in-home consultation online or visit one of its eleven showrooms.

For president and CEO Ted Sherritt, productivity improvements have been a priority in two areas: processes at the shop level, where product is manufactured, and at the field level, where a significant part of the company's business is generated by more than 150 staff taking orders and then templating and installing countertops in the kitchens of customers.

"A big part of 'lean' is staff engagement," says Sherritt, a CA and CBV who came to FLOFORM in 1995 as vice-president of finance from a major accounting and audit firm. ("This is way more fun," he says.) "Getting our people trained and engaged in productivity has been very successful. They're the people on the floor, and they have by far the best ideas on eliminating waste." At the plant level, those improvements have been made by changing the physical layout, rearranging equipment so that there is physically less distance to cover (and less time wasted) as a job moves from one step to another. Gains have also been made with employee input by streamlining processing—reducing a process that once took sixteen steps to thirteen, for example.

The most striking productivity improvement has come through implementing new technology with templating and installation staff that has yielded radically more efficient processes. In the old system, a staff member would visit a home to take measurements for a new kitchen counter, for example. He or she would measure the counter sections required and create a cardboard template. As anyone who has ever measured anything in a typical North American home knows, nothing can ever be counted on to be square or level. Customer satisfaction thus was highly dependent on the staff person being capable with a tape measure, cutting tool, and cardboard in creating the life-size template.

Once a week, FLOFORM would ship, via one of its own delivery trucks, templates from the sales offices and take them to one of its two fabricating locations, Saskatoon and Seattle, where the templates would be digitized in order to allow CNC (computer numerically controlled) equipment to make a precise finished product. Under such a paradigm of efficiency, running a truck once a week represented sound business practice, as running a truck daily with a limited number of orders would be inefficient in terms of driver time, fuel consumption, and vehicle maintenance and depreciation. But weekly deliveries helped ensure that it might take at best ten days to complete an order.

The first step in improving FLOFORM's productivity was to get rid of the time wasted transporting the cardboard templates. Digitization was shifted to the company's eleven sales and showroom locations, which could then send the CNC-ready file electronically to one of the fabricating shops. Getting cardboard off the road, and taking back the time lost in organizing their shipments to the shops along a weekly schedule, was a great leap forward in productivity. But it left two critical steps. The installation staff in the field were still creating cardboard templates and driving them to a sales office. And at the sales office, someone was still digitizing the physical template. FLOFORM was measuring twice to cut once— in the house, and then at the sales office. Measuring the cardboard template to make a digital file, in addition to consuming more time and requiring more labour, also presented an opportunity for error. In constructing countertops, errors are fairly unforgiving, because if the fit is wrong it can be difficult if not impossible to alter the delivered product. Waste then is compounded. All the time, labour, and materials from the original effort is discarded, the process has to start over again, and the reputation of the company has been negatively impacted if an error has caused the delay of an entire kitchen renovation.

FLOFORM began introducing its solution in 2009 and completed the rollout in the field in 2011. Staff were now equipped with a portable digitizing tool that could measure and create the final electronic template right in the customer's kitchen, without any cardboard. That template could then be e-mailed directly to the fabricating shop. The field staff was now measuring once—precisely and carefully—and the shop was cutting once. Opportunities for error in creating a template were halved. The sales staff had also begun to carry the showroom with them in a laptop or a tablet, as the customer could inspect the company product line in their kitchen, on the company website.

"There's no cardboard travelling down the highway anymore," says Sherritt. "The guy in the house now has the most important job because we don't change the specifications once he has created the digital template. He's also now one of the most skilled people we've got."

The digitization tool FLOFORM now provides to the templating staff costs about $20,000 per unit. But this investment more than pays for itself in productivity gains. "We can have a customer make a rush order on a Monday and have it installed on a Wednesday. It's much improved our turnaround time and our quality, and that's eliminating waste." Because of the new process's speed and accuracy, says Sherritt, "one person in the field can create templates for three or four homes in a single day, instead of two. We're getting rid of all that time invested in making and shipping cardboard, and we're so much closer to a final product. It probably represents a 33 to 50 percent improvement in productivity."

● ● ●

In 1978, Gord Wiebe (who is today CEO), Harry Buhler, and Henry Banman established All Weather Windows in Edmonton in a ten-thousand-square-foot manufacturing facility with just nine employees. It took only two years of sales growth to compel them to move into a thirty-five-thousand-square-foot plant. More than thirty years later, All Weather Windows has almost four hundred thousand square feet of manufacturing capacity in two locations, Edmonton and Mississauga, with a workforce of about a thousand.

Since 2006, the company has been increasing productivity through a lean manufacturing initiative that has transformed how All Weather Windows manufactures its product and views its relationships with its customers and its own workforce.

All Weather Windows is an excellent example of a company that approaches lean manufacturing from a starting point of customer needs. Everything from the design of innovative products, to manufacturing set-ups, to the drive to improve ordering and delivery times, derives from understanding the key factors of the customers' satisfaction. As a company pursues improvements to increase satisfaction, it forces waste out of the manufacturing and servicing process.

All Weather Windows has defied the general weakness Canadian companies have shown in investing in machinery and equipment. "We have invested heavily in them to minimize labour costs," says Richard Scott, who was vice-president of plant operations when he joined All Weather Windows in 2005 and launched the lean production initiative. Now president, Scott states: "We're no longer about guys with hammers. Our manufacturing has become highly automated."

True to the general objective of improving labour productivity, All Weather Windows has sought gains by leveraging the investment in equipment. "There are fewer people," says Scott, "but we have a more highly paid technical staff." All Weather Windows is more competitive, and as an employer it is offering better-paying jobs that benefit the general economy. Scott says the window business faces pressures from manufacturing beyond our borders that employs cheaper labour, but the solution has been shifting to better-paid, more-skilled workers who can produce product that meets rigid Canadian standards, particularly in energy efficiency.

V-weld technology, introduced in 2010, has proved to be a significant differentiator. With this new technology, combination windows are welded together, virtually eliminating any air or water leaks. With V-weld, a combination window will test to the same performance as a single operating window, delivering better structural and energy efficiency performance than other combination windows. The capital equipment and development investment has been significant, but the company sees substantial long-term benefits in product performance leadership, increased capacity, and overall reduction of labour and material costs, not to mention increased customer satisfaction.

Automation means that All Weather Windows requires fewer manual processes to produce its windows and doors, which in turn means lower defect rates and higher productivity. The chief benefit of lower defect rates is higher customer satisfaction. While "satisfaction" might seem an intangible concept, All Weather Windows quantifies customer satisfaction with a dashboard program that tracks performance for individual clients using such metrics as order delivery, order fill rate, and product quality.

Satisfaction is especially important in a business that relies on contractors and retailers to represent its product to consumers. A home owner may only buy replacement windows once, and if a manufacturer has a 5 percent defect rate, this customer is statistically more than likely to be satisfied with a purchase. A repeat customer like a retailer or a contractor is less likely to be contented when one in twenty windows has a problem. Defects produce headaches with their own dissatisfied customers as well as delays in completing projects. All else being equal, these customers will take their business to the supplier with a defect rate of one in thirty or forty, or better. In their world, small statistical improvements in quality mean significant differences in dissatisfaction levels. A reduction in error from 5 percent to 2.5 percent means there are half as many problem windows for them to deal with on a volume basis. (All Weather Windows' defect rate is actually much lower.) Small wonder that companies like All Weather Windows, seeking a competitive advantage in a highly competitive industry, rely on lean production principles to improve productivity even slightly.

The company uses lean discipline to measure, monitor, and reduce post-production defect rates. Measuring this way allows All Weather Windows to distinguish between defects due to their production processes and damage that might incur in shipping, which can be better investigated and eliminated.

All Weather Windows is not alone in recognizing that customers want higher quality and shorter lead times, as retailers and contractors pursue just-in-time efficiencies in satisfying their own clients. All Weather Windows' customer might be the order desk at a consumer retail outlet, which in turn has customers who don't have the patience for protracted order fulfillment when they can get something more quickly elsewhere. That customer can also be a contractor renovating a multi-unit residential building, as All Weather Windows' commercial arm has benefited from a boom in the revitalization of residential buildings in downtown cores.

"A lot of older buildings are being retrofitted," says Scott. "Part of our mission statement is to produce energy-efficient products," which is what these projects often demand.

The rallying cry at All Weather Windows has become "on time and complete." As Scott explains: "Every morning, our discussion is safety, then quality, then 'on-time and complete.' To us, that doesn't mean when something is finished at the plant. It's when it's delivered to the customer. It's not good enough if it's finished in the plant and sitting there for three days. Our target is a maximum of ten working days from the time of order placement to delivery to the customer, so we make sure some of our capacity exceeds our demand. No one wants to wait anymore."

Manufacturing efficiency used to be thought of along the Model-T line. A manufacturer strove to tool up for long runs of a product with little to no variation that would inhibit uninterrupted production. Henry Ford famously offered the Model T in any colour, so long as it was black. Such manufacturing rigidity is impossible in the window business. While All Weather Windows produces a variety of specific designs, the marketplace is extremely unpredictable in its short-term demands. The old-economy solution of inventory stockpiling is unworkable, but having production capacity always at hand to meet all possible product demands is wasteful.

The solution All Weather Windows adopted in its lean manufacturing is a "product platform strategy." Products are set on one of three common platforms, on which a variety of different windows can be built. "It can happen that nobody wants sliders this week, and everybody wants casements," says Scott. "We can now convert lines in two hours. In the past, all the product manufacturing lines used to be different. Ours are now on common equipment using common product components as part of the platform strategy. We're also one of the few manufacturers with its production facilities tied together. We can produce at both plants and manage capacity utilization."

Richard Scott stresses that a chief benefit of lean manufacturing is that "you end up with an engaged workforce. 'Lean' for us is a culture. It's top-down in support, but it's bottom-up in the way innovation and sustainability come from our people. Our people know where they stand and can come back with suggestions for improving productivity and processes. We've seen improvement all across our lines, and they've come from our employees."

● ● ●

Located in Altona, Manitoba, Friesens Corporation has a history
that stretches back to 1907, when David W. Friesen bought a
small confectionery store in the Mennonite community. In 1927,
he bought a local bookstore and added a small letterpress printing
press in 1933. With that press, the first local newspaper, the *Red
River Valley Echo*, was established in 1941. After the war, the
family-owned company moved to employee profit-sharing as it
grew and entered the printing business for book publishing in
the 1980s. Today, Friesens employs more than five hundred people
at its Altona facility and is one of Canada's largest independent
book manufacturers, with about 30 percent of its business coming
from the United States. It is renowned for quality, having won
more than fifty Printing Industry of America awards over the last
decade.

While the rise of e-books has inspired many predictions of the
death of print, the book remains a marvel as a way to package and
transport human thought and imagery, and seems to have a greater
future than is routinely forecast.

"Graphic novels are doing very well in print," says Curwin
Friesen, who has been CEO since 2007. "Physicality is part of the
product. We've been focusing more on coffee-table books, museum
books, and high-end art books. But whatever happens to books, we
have to be the most efficient and productive printer that we can be."

Indeed, the worst strategy that a typical printer could adapt in
the face of rising popularity of e-books is to take refuge in a notion
of printing as a tradecraft process. There may be fewer printers
around as time progresses, but the competitive climate is only going
to increase. Friesens already rose to and met the challenge in quality
colour printing posed in the 1990s by firms in Europe and Asia.

It continues to strive to improve productivity by approaching the challenge through lean manufacturing principles.

In publishing, the printing process is the end of the line in turning a manuscript into a physical book. It is also the last stage of the process to have been transformed digitally. Writers and editors have long changed to word processors for writing and to a large degree for editing. Typesetting, design, illustration, and photography have migrated substantially to the digital world of software. Even with text-based books, page proofs or galleys are largely circulated now digitally, in PDF files.

"When I joined Friesens in 1996," Curwin Friesen recalls, "people talked about printing as an art form." Where colour printing was concerned, it was about a press operator setting up for a print run and tinkering with the machine's colour settings to match a physical proof that had been approved by the client. "It's nice to still think of printing as an art, but we're competing against low-cost competitors. The focus now is on manufacturing. It's the definition of what we do."

Friesens approaches productivity improvement from three interrelated angles: lean manufacturing, automation, and employee cross-training.

Every year, Friesens holds a Print Fair during which the plant at Altona is shut down for a full day to allow the staff to attend training sessions that include guest speakers on an array of topics. In 2010, Friesens brought in a NASCAR professional to speak about the ceaseless drive for efficiency in pit crews. By closely analyzing every step in a particular task, crews are able to shave precious seconds off routines that make the difference between winning and losing when cars travel at speeds of over 300 kilometres per hour and sitting still in the pit is time and distance lost. The staff was told how one routine was reduced from sixty to forty-five seconds, and even though no one thought it could ever possibly be done more quickly than thirty seconds, the process was ultimately slashed to fourteen seconds. "It happens because you measure everything and drive every second out of the process that you can," Friesen says.

A colour press is not a stock car, but it is a sophisticated piece of machinery and part of a workflow process in which time is money. Friesens is in constant pursuit of lean manufacturing, aiming to produce high-quality work with minimal waste. "You drive out waste," Friesen says, "and waste is time and materials."

Friesens considers itself to be in the custom manufacturing business. "We don't set up a chocolate bar line and then run Snickers for years." Books have certain shared parameters in how pages are printed in sheets and are then trimmed and bound, for example, but they're all as unique as the words and images within them. "Every order is different, and it's not for inventory." Friesens has had to figure out how to bring increasing efficiency to a process that must adapt to the specifics of every order.

"We've digitized the pre-press," says Friesen. "Now we need to ask: 'How quickly should we set up colour?' We define parameters that productivity has to be hitting. We say, 'you've got six minutes to set up the colour percentages on the press.'"

The printing process has two "ends." The "front end," called pre-press, is where a job arrives from a client and is prepared for the press. The "back end" is where the book becomes an object, on the press and in the bindery. The front end is the aspect of printing that underwent the greatest initial change, as physical layouts gave way to digital files. Clients upload files containing book page layouts to the pre-press department and then inspect digital proofs online, although some still request physical, paper proofs as well.

For both printer and client, corrections take time, and time is money. Clients are generally doing their own software-driven file verifications prior to uploading, but Friesens has been increasing its speed-of-response in checking files for problems as soon as they arrive. Mistakes do get made, with image resolution, fonts, and pictures mistakenly left in an RGB (red-green-blue) computer-monitor colour specification rather than the CMYK (cyan-magenta-yellow-black) format a press requires, to name a few typical hazards. It can be critical to catch these errors immediately and let the client know as soon as possible that there is a problem to be remedied. "We want to minimize 'touch time.' We want the computer to process jobs in minutes at pre-press, not in days. We can give a customer instantaneous response to issues in a file. You don't want to wait two weeks to find out there's a problem in what you submitted."

Any delays at pre-press can be catastrophic when speed-to-market is critical. During the 2010 Winter Olympics in Vancouver, Friesens was printing "instant" books for clients who needed to capitalize on the public interest before it faded. "We were trying to get books out four to five days after events had happened. We can't take six, eight, ten weeks in a situation like that."

Such speed is possible, says Friesen, because "we've built automation at the back end. Pre-press, at the front end, used to be our largest department. Now it's one of the smallest." As efficiencies have transformed the front end, "we've sped up the process at the press." A new, state-of-the-art digital press was added in 2010. "We don't use colour proofs anymore, even though some customers still ask for them. We match colour on highly calibrated screens right at the press, where proofing by the client is shown. We're using software workflow and training press operators to get the on-screen representation of the digital proof onto the printed page."

Friesens has become especially determined to reduce material waste. Just one of Friesens' four large-format presses can output up to 5 tonnes of paper in a single day. Printing presses run through paper in test runs as colour for a particular job is calibrated. The company tracks and weighs the amount of paper consumed in every job. "If our wastage is 5 percent, we ask: 'What about 4 percent?' We look at the yield of books from paper. A lot of our productivity effort in recent years has gone into waste reduction and monitoring. We're trying to run faster, with less waste."

Friesens has turned to cross-training employees to improve productivity in the way labour is deployed. With each job being a custom order, volumes and types of work change unpredictably. There can be more output in hardcover than paperback in the bindery, for example. "We get peaks and valleys all the time. Things are streaming through the plant in very lumpy ways. We use labour as efficiently as possible to drive productivity." Employees are trained with multiple skill sets so they can be allocated appropriately to address workflow bottlenecks. "We even take people from pre-press and put them on the press." By moving people between different cost centres, Friesens improves productivity by the raw measure of the number of people required to produce a certain number of books.

"We need to do more with the same or less," Curwin Friesen says. "That has to be the central point of manufacturing."

●  ●  ●

Productivity is a commitment to never-ending improvement in the value of output achieved from labour. We have seen at Friesens how some improvements are incremental, the equivalent of the stock-car pit crew analyzing steps in a process to squeeze out precious seconds of wasted motion. Other improvements require major changes in methodology or production, as FLOFORM has shown with its new approach to measuring counters in the field, which are often driven by new technology that minimizes the engagement of human hands with a process to reduce time and error. Still others require innovation in products to improve manufacturing efficiency and the value proposition to the customer. Productivity is a branch of innovation in which seemingly small improvements in a statistic like defects or on-time delivery can yield significant competitive advantages. All Weather Windows for one has recognized that seemingly small improvements pay major dividends in customer satisfaction, as the company looks downstream not only to the needs of its customers, but to the needs of the customers of its customers.

While we have focused on companies in manufacturing in this chapter, the concept of productivity applies to all business disciplines, services included. Because it is a process rather than a patentable property, productivity is also open to all enterprises to exploit. To rank among Canada's Best Managed Companies, productivity must be relentlessly pursued, because the competition is also sure to be doing so. For Canada, that is a good thing. A rising tide of productivity will lift all boats, as the country closes the gap with its fellow leading industrial nations.

# 12

# SUCCESSION: LOOKING BEYOND TODAY'S OWNERS AND MANAGERS

In March 2007, M. Sullivan & Son of Arnprior, Ontario, one of the largest family-owned general contractors in Canada, reached a crossroads, if not a crisis point. Mort Sullivan, one of three sons of founder Maurice Sullivan who had started the business in 1914, passed away at age ninety-four. Mere months earlier, his nephew Eric too had passed away. Until those deaths, M. Sullivan had been run by the triumvirate of Mort and his nephews Eric and Tommy on behalf of shareholders in the Sullivan family. There was no real board, and Mort Sullivan had served as an ad hoc CEO while Tommy Sullivan took care of day-to-day business. Now, with Mort and Eric suddenly gone, the responsibility for running this major general contractor fell to Tommy, who was seventy-six and had been working for the company since he began hauling bricks at age sixteen.

There wasn't an obvious successor to Tommy, either in the family's fourth generation or the company's management ranks. All at once, M. Sullivan was in urgent need of succession planning. While active family management would end after three generations, the company was enjoying its strongest years, and with more than two hundred employees, it felt obligations to more than the family shareholders to carry on. The question was whether M. Sullivan could do everything necessary to put its own management and processes on a secure footing before time ran out.

● ● ●

Succession planning is—or should be—a front-burner issue for Canada's privately held companies. About one-third of independent business owners intend to exit their enterprises in the next five years, but many of them will fail to arrange an orderly transition. All too often, the issue goes unaddressed and the planning is left far too late. Owners become "stuck"—unable to leave when they want. In the worst-case scenario, a proprietor is never able to retire, and either the proprietor or his or her estate is forced to wind up the business without realizing any of the intangible value built up over what may have been decades, even generations. Alternatively, businesses are sold for far less than what they could have garnered, or they quickly falter through poorly or hastily conceived succession plans that alienate customers and key employees alike.

In this chapter, we meet three companies that have grappled with the challenges of succession. M. Sullivan & Son is one of them, a thriving enterprise that found itself at the brink of succession difficulties and rapidly—and successfully—began planning its way out of them. Our other profiled companies reveal how strong succession planning can be not years but decades in the making.

As we'll see, succession planning, which focuses on the change in ownership, is inseparable from transition planning, which is an ongoing process that takes a holistic view of the business as well as the owner. Transition planning involves building a sustainable business by focusing on creating and protecting value. Without transition planning, a business will be hard-pressed to endure a change in ownership. A business's ownership may also fail to identify succession options within its management ranks; at the least, it will jeopardize any hope of a smooth ownership succession by alienating the organization.

Every company faces a unique set of succession circumstances. Some are particular to (even endemic within) an industry. As we saw in Chapter 1, "Strategy: Brewing Up a Winning Formula for Marketplace Success," succession problems were so widespread among Canadian veterinary clinics that they provided an opportunity for an entirely new business model, that of Associate Veterinary Clinics, to arise as an exit solution. Many private enterprises are held by families, which struggle with succession from many perspectives. Some of these families want to turn the enterprise over to a succeeding generation, but lack family members with the necessary talent, experience, and ambition. Some of these families have a surplus of candidates, and their differences can cause destabilizing antagonism.

The options typically involve trade-offs. The highest return usually comes from selling to a strategic buyer, followed by a sale to management and financial investors, with generational transfer achieving the lowest valuations. The best tax efficiency opportunities, however, tend to be available with generational transfer to family members. Tax planning considerations, in turn, include income taxes on death, capital gains exemptions, and estate freezes. Generational transfers tend to have the least complexity, with successions becoming increasingly complicated given the alternatives of a management buyout, sale of the business, or an IPO.

Succession is a rare area of professional business advice that must answer to strong emotional prerogatives. For many family enterprises, pride in the business and a desire for continuity through future generations can outweigh strict material analysis of the financial consequences of succession options. For example, it may be impossible for owners to think of an enterprise (with the family name on it) that was founded by a grandparent being run by anyone other than a family member.

For M. Sullivan & Co., succession planning came to a head in the most trying way possible: the deaths of two of the three key family members who had long been running it.

M. Sullivan & Son was founded in 1914 by Maurice Sullivan. After his death in 1938, the company was run by his sons, Dominique, Mort, and Harry. Tommy and Eric Sullivan, sons of Harry, also joined the business. By 2006, management was the responsibility of Mort and his nephews Tommy and Eric. As noted, the passing of Mort and Eric then forced the family's investors to come to grips with the future of their company, being run at the time by seventy-six-year-old Tommy.

M. Sullivan first established a formal board, with three external and two internal directors. The board then went looking for a successor for Tommy. As Tommy Sullivan was chair of the board, he was active in seeking his own replacement. In 2008, M. Sullivan secured its first outside president and CEO, Robert (Bob) MacLaren, who knew the company well from his time at Hydro One Networks and Ontario Power Generation. In particular, as project manager for eastern Ontario at OPG he had dealt with M. Sullivan when putting out tenders. MacLaren in turn was one of those many personal contacts Tommy Sullivan had built up over the decades in running the company. As MacLaren would say of him, Tommy "built lifelong relationships with contractors, suppliers, architects, associations, clients, and competitors alike. Thanks to Tommy Sullivan, many of the company's most fruitful relationships have spanned four, five, and even six decades, with mutual respect leading to mutual benefit on all sides."

When MacLaren arrived, Tommy Sullivan didn't entirely withdraw from the business. "He stepped back a little bit, but he liked to maintain some involvement," says MacLaren. "He had a major influence as chair of the board of directors." When Tommy Sullivan passed away in January 2012, the last link to the Sullivan family in the active management of the namesake company was broken. By then, the family's shareholders were already taking further steps to plan for the company's future.

"The board is now in process of defining how it is going to operate for the next ten years," says MacLaren. "We're revisiting mandate and function. We're also bringing more independent people on board." The board is asking for a comprehensive succession plan for senior management. "We do have a succession plan for myself in place," MacLaren explains. "The next step is to develop a plan for the CFO and other members of the senior management team."

M. Sullivan's succession and transition planning has never stopped since the passing of Mort Sullivan in 2007 forced the company to confront a future without strong leadership and clear governance. The company now follows a three-year business plan, for example, that is reviewed with the board of directors—one of a number of changes that has led it to being named one of Canada's Best Managed Companies.

● ● ●

We advise business owners that succession and transition planning has three stages. They need to develop a transition plan, execute a business plan and monitor its progress, and then prepare for and execute the ownership transition. The existence of a strong management team and corporate governance regime will increase the value of the business materially.

The transition plan requires them to determine their business and personal goals. Do they plan on immediate retirement or to have some continuing role in the business? Do they want to invest in another enterprise? They need a realistic estimate of what the business is worth. A timeline is also crucial, not only for the immediate process of succession, which can take anywhere from three months for a generational transfer to a year or more for an IPO, but for preparing the business.

A business plan ensures the value of the enterprise is optimized to realize the highest return. In monitoring its progress, the owner needs to be asking if the business is increasing in value and identifying the risks to that value. He or she has to be able to show why a third party would want to buy the business, if that is the option. Whatever succession course is chosen, a strong management team and corporate governance regimen should be in place.

Lastly, the owner has to be prepared to execute the succession transaction. This requires a strong grasp of cash needs for retirement, necessary tax and estate plans, and financing necessary to buy out partners if that becomes part of the business's succession scenario. There is more than one way to exit a business, and the final choice should maximize value. Every owner will measure that value a different way, according to his or her own needs, continuation of the enterprise, estate planning, and the nature of the desired or available transition model.

If a generational transfer or management buyout is contemplated, years of preparation may be warranted, both for mentoring the new ownership and leaders and for ensuring a stable transition for the organization as a whole. Succession and transition in fact can be a front-burner issue throughout the working life of a business owner. Winnipeg's Vector Construction Group is a prime example. The company was practically founded with a succession plan in place.

● ● ●

Vector Construction Group was established in 1965 by three men as G.M.W. Ltd. "My partners were significantly older than I was," says Donald (Don) Whitmore, a professional engineer. "It was understood that as the years went on and the business became established, I would take over." In 1979, Whitmore did just that, buying out his partners and going solo.

The company had started out in heavy construction, tackling jobs like highway grading, dam building, and site development. In the last few years of the original partnership, Manitoba Hydro had become a client. Soon after Whitmore bought out his partners, Manitoba Hydro came to him with a job proposition. The provincial hydroelectric utility liked the quality of Whitmore's work and the integrity of his operation. It had an important project it wanted him to take on: refurbishing the concrete dam at the Seven Sisters Generating Station.

Located about 90 kilometres east of Winnipeg on the Winnipeg River, Seven Sisters—named for seven rapids along 11 kilometres of white water—had grown to six turbines producing 500 megawatts of power through construction projects that stretched from 1929 to 1952. In 1979, the Seven Sisters' earliest construction reached the half-century mark. The utility planned a major, six-year rehabilitation project to extend its productive life another fifty years. Winter freezing and thawing had seriously damaged the concrete structure, and Manitoba Hydro invited Whitmore to take on the refurbishment.

Whitmore had never dealt with concrete rehabilitation. But he accepted the opportunity and hired the talent he needed to repair Seven Sisters. "Not only did I have the challenge of being the one owner, but now we were diversifying." Because of the Seven Sisters project, which Whitmore brought in under budget and ahead of schedule and earned Vector the Concrete Repair Institute Award of Excellence for Longevity, his company had a new focus. Concrete repair and restoration remains the core enterprise in Vector Construction Group and drove the company's expansion from its headquarters in Winnipeg.

After buying out his original partners, succession planning was on Don Whitmore's mind "virtually from the get-go." The issue could not be left to address at his convenience. Construction is a capital-intensive business. "Bankers and bonding companies want to know 'what if,'" says Whitmore, and from the beginning he had to have an answer for them. (Bob MacLaren notes that the queries of bonding companies also accelerated the succession planning process at M. Sullivan & Son.)

Part of that succession planning involved Don Whitmore's son David, who was just completing his engineering studies when the company shifted into concrete restoration. David spent summer hours on Vector projects, and as soon as his engineering studies were done, he enrolled in an MBA program.

"When he finished the MBA, we had a discussion," says Don Whitmore. David Whitmore would have to prove himself if he hoped to take over the company some day. "Entitlement didn't cut it." David Whitmore did prove himself, by spearheading the expansion to Thunder Bay, southern Ontario, and Saskatchewan.

The entire time, a succession plan was in place, which was more complicated than a generational change in authority and ownership. "I didn't build this business singlehanded," says Don

Whitmore. "I started telling employees years ago that if my obituary appeared in the paper, there weren't any worries for them." In the event of Whitmore's demise, in the immediate term an insurance policy funded a shareholder agreement and would also ensure that there was no negative cash impact on the operation due to his passing.

Such an insurance-based transition plan still exists. The main difference between the start of Don Whitmore's succession planning and the company's present situation is that the next generation now has two participants, president David Whitmore and his brother-in-law, Bob Spriggs, who is CEO. (Don Whitmore continues as chair.) David Whitmore and Bob Spriggs in turn have their own ownership agreement and insurance. Their children range in age from twelve to twenty-two, with no successor ready to take the reins. "If the company goes further, to a third generation, then great," says Spriggs. "If not, then we'll look at alternatives." The brothers-in-law make it a policy never to travel together, and in the event of their passing, the agreement and insurance will allow Vector to continue operating. So-called "key-man" insurance will fund the process of finding executive replacements for them, as well as pay any taxes due. "It will be up to the company to find replacements for us and to carry forward," says Spriggs.

Such lifetime-of-company attention to succession and transition planning has also been central to the success of Western Sales, a major player in agricultural equipment sales in west-central Saskatchewan. It began with a small shop in Rosetown established by Glen Thresher, which was awarded a John Deere dealership in 1947. In 1954, Fred Friend arrived as sales manager; after Thresher's death in 1965, Friend bought the dealership in 1966. Western Sales carried forward under the ownership of the Friend family, expanding first 40 kilometres south to Elrose. Fred Friend retired in 1979, and his sons took over the business, led by Doug Friend. By 1980, Western Sales was the largest John Deere dealership in Canada, a distinction it held for three years, and it remains one of the largest in the country.

While Western Sales had become a family business with the Friends, there was no plan to make it a multi-generational enterprise. In 1985, Doug Friend brought Grant McGrath into the business. Friend was only in his thirties, but he was already set to retire. "He took a chance on a guy twenty-four, twenty-five years old," says McGrath. The following year, McGrath and two partners bought shares from one of the Friend brothers.

The company next went 60 kilometres north of Rosetown to add a branch in Biggar in 1988. Outlook, about 70 kilometres east, was added in 1991. At the time, its four branches made Western Sales the John Deere dealership with the largest geographical area in Canada. It would expand again in 2007, with an acquisition of an existing dealer operation that added branches in Davidson, 140 kilometres east of Rosetown, and Central Butte, about 130 kilometres southeast of Rosetown.

As time passed, Grant McGrath acquired more of the equity from his two partners, and in 2000 became president and general manager. By 2008, he was the sole proprietor. Today, Western Sales employs about 125 people in its six locations. The business has grown beyond selling and servicing the big machinery like combines and tractors relied on by grain farmers to seed, spray, and harvest. Farmers now turn to Western Sales as well for fieldSMART, a new company created by Western Sales, that enables producers to utilize the information and technology of today's sophisticated farm equipment to manage data and make sound decisions using a team of professional agronomists.

"As I was growing my company, adding branches," says

McGrath, "I saw the need for Western Sales to be secure, not only in the eyes of the community but where the needs of employees are concerned. Any succession has to be done on a solid foundation." He could not afford to leave it to the last minute. The large-equipment business in Western Canada unfortunately is full of owners who have reached sixty without crafting any succession plan and with few options before them.

Like Doug Friend before him, McGrath began looking for his successors while he was still relatively young, in this case in his forties. McGrath planned to bring them along within the organization and turn over day-to-day operations long before he had any intention of retiring. He found his succession candidates in Carl Persson and Jason Hintze, young men who had grown up in Western Sales' territory and were passionate about the business. "When I was seventeen," says Persson, "I wanted to be a John Deere dealer."

Jason Hintze, now forty, had left Elrose to attend university and after graduation had gone to work for McGrath at Western Sales in 1994. He moved into the sales department in 1996 as a sales representative, rising to general sales manager in 2001. Persson, thirty-six, had grown up on a family farm in the Rosetown area and after obtaining an engineering degree had entered heavy equipment sales with a rival to John Deere. Persson had known Western Sales from the family farm, and he and McGrath stayed in touch. "We played cat and mouse for about ten years," says Persson. "I'd say, 'What are you doing?' He'd say, 'What are *you* doing?'" At last, in 2008, Persson joined Western Sales as aftermarket manager and became vice-president of operations in 2011.

McGrath planned for Hintze and Persson to assume the leadership of the company, but when Persson arrived, it was understood there would be a two-year trial to ensure he and Hintze could work together and that they were prepared for the demands of a partnership. "Being a partner, the job never really does leave you," says McGrath. "It takes a special person to do that." Once Hintze and Persson had proved they were an effective team, a succession structure was put in place in 2010.

McGrath has no plans on exiting, and at the moment he retains 90 percent of the equity. "I like my company and the people I'm associated with. I want to continue that relationship and will continue as president and CEO. I'm not big on titles, though. I will continue to have a hand in the business. But in terms of day-to-day management, it's important there are people on the ground to handle things."

"My succession plan is not all about retirement or selling," McGrath emphasizes. "It's about accelerating corporate value, with a succession of operational leadership that has ownership. This new leadership will make Western Sales stronger." McGrath says the Western Sales ownership strategy is creating a model for a future acquisition opportunity, as he is a shareholder in another four-store John Deere organization in southern Alberta that is following the same ownership strategy. The approach is allowing McGrath "to work on the vision and strategic planning for growth opportunities."

Finding the right people to assume operational leadership at Western Sales, and eventually its ownership, was complicated by the demographics of rural Saskatchewan. The communities are small. Elrose has fewer than 500 people; Rosetown has 2300. The largest city in the province, Saskatoon, about 110 kilometres northeast of Rosetown, is 220,000 strong. And Saskatchewan's population had shrunk by 1 percent between 1996 and 2006, as young people sought opportunities elsewhere. The province rebounded dramatically between 2006 and 2011, its population growing by almost 7 percent to surpass one million for the first time since 1986, but that population growth had been driven not by rural agriculture but by the natural resources boom to the north.

Western Sales found its new generation of owners locally, just as it continues to cultivate its workforce, including its future managers, in the small communities of its branches. "In any organization, culture defines success and the potential for growth," says McGrath. "People who embrace that are essential for continuity and growth. I've found over the years that we have a unique culture in west-central Saskatchewan. We are fortunate that we have very talented local people graduating from university and technical programs who we can bring into our organization. It's much easier bringing people into the fold if they've been born into the culture." Culture matching, as we saw in Chapter 6 ("Mergers and Acquisitions: Making Instead of Breaking by Matching Cultures") and Chapter 10 ("Attracting and Retaining Talent: Building the Lattice"), is a priority that cuts across a variety of management priorities. For Western Sales, finding the talent the company requires day-to-day, as well as in the long term where succession is concerned, has relied on a culture inextricably tied to the land that its customers plant and harvest.

"Rosetown is an hour and ten minutes from Saskatoon," says Persson. "It's not a twenty-minute drive down the road to get whatever you want. People really have to want the lifestyle of a small rural community. It's important that we find the people who are comfortable in a small town. We've tried to pull in people from the Toronto area as technicians, but it's just not a good fit. We want to bring in young people who are tied to the community and have them grow into managers. When middle managers retire, we need to have those young people in position to take their place. We have a policy that every manager needs to be looking for his or her replacement."

Adds McGrath: "We bring young people in from high school, treat them right, train them, and groom them to move up the ladder." Western Sales has turned to Executive Source Partners of Regina, an executive search and leadership consulting firm, for help in building its management and sales teams. Executive Source Partners uses The Attentional and Interpersonal Style Inventory (TAIS) evaluation methodology. "We work closely with them," says McGrath, "identifying performance qualities for different roles. There's a science to it. We're up to 125 people now, and it's a big part of what we do."

Considering the elements that have made for a successful succession plan at Western Sales, McGrath can point to his decision to start preparing when he was relatively young, just as Doug Friend did before him. He also recognized that there was more to succession than cash. In fact, the Western Sales example makes an important distinction between a pure exit strategy—sell the business for as much as you can—and a business transition plan. In the latter case, it is critical to choose people carefully. They need to maintain the winning culture of the organization as well as its profitability. They also need to be groomed, which takes time, and that means they're invariably young, just as McGrath was when he got his chance under Doug Friend.

"Often, talent, age, and financial status don't come in the same package," says McGrath. "I found younger men than me who had all kinds of talent but maybe not the cash to invest at the level the company is worth. But you structure a succession properly, there are a lot of ways to bring talented people into an organization."

Transition planning in truth is never-ending. To maximize value for the present ownership, the organization must be constantly grooming its own leaders to the ultimate benefit of future owners, who may not even have been identified yet. Like Western Sales,

Vector Construction Group looks to its employee ranks for a new generation of leaders. "Initially, the company was much more an owner-operator structure," says Don Whitmore. "In the early years it was like a wheel on a Red River cart. I was the hub and the spokes led to where the wheel was in the mud, doing the work. In the late 1990s, there was a major structural reorganization. It's now very flat, with some hierarchy of business divisions."

In 2011, Vector created its own leadership development program, one that is true to the company's operating framework and values. That year, 160 staff went through the program, and a further round of training was planned for more staff in 2012.

"We invest significantly to prepare future leaders," says Bob Spriggs. Technical and safety training are common in organizations, he says, but not personal growth and development. Vector uses Myers-Briggs Type Indicator (MBTI) psychometric program as a tool to allow participants "to learn more about yourself as an individual," says Spriggs. "It aids in communication, in identifying roles and responsibilities, and what would be more attractive to them."

Spriggs is proud of the fact that the company has low personnel turnover. "In construction, turnover can be very high. We like to promote and move people within. No matter what position you're in, you need to be ID-ing people who can take your job so you can move to different things. Were something to happen to Don, Dave, or myself, this company has people who are very capable of moving things forward."

"We've always had a plan for calamity or disaster if someone is incapacitated or lost," says Don Whitmore. "We're big on backup and succession all down through divisions. To me, succession planning is never-ending. I started thinking about it years before all the agreements and structures were in place. And the second generation is making its own plans, with structure and insurance."

In 2008, the Canadian Association of Family Enterprise (CAFE) named Vector its Manitoba family enterprise of the year and a national finalist, a testament in part to its rigorous succession planning. Spriggs says, "It's one of the things you can't start too early. You've got to table those discussions, whether the successor is another member of the family or not. If you leave it too late, it's decided for you. You need to talk about these things, or you'll run into a lot of problems. You have to involve key advisors, people you trust, to help with items that need to be discussed. We may think up 90 percent of them, but advisors have interesting takes that need to be considered."

M. Sullivan & Son was able to overcome the succession adversity created by the rapid loss of key senior people. The lesson for other family-owned companies, says Robert MacLaren, is that they should be addressing succession sooner rather than later, as Western Sales and Vector Construction Group did. "It's not easy because you're looking at your own mortality, but business interests have to be paramount. Everybody has to have an exit strategy, and that has to be based on good business decisions." That strategy may not have a practical role for another generation of owner-managers. "The further you get from the founder, the more diluted and complex the family ownership becomes in individual owners. Selling to employees or outside investors are options that should be explored."

And especially where a succession plan involving a family is concerned, that process cannot forget about the employees who need certainty about their own careers and welfare. "How do you prepare the organization for that change?" Vector's Bob Spriggs proposes: "Is it expecting dramatic change? You don't want to shock the system."

Succession planning is far more complex than identifying and preparing a new generation of senior management or choosing the most advantageous way of transferring in the equity in the company. Once the present ownership has identified its objectives, the focus must turn to optimizing the company's value.

We see value being achieved in four areas: revenue, operating margin, financial leverage, and capability and sustainability. To achieve revenue goals, the company needs to win market share from competitors, expand its customer base, protect against new market entrants, and improve its product quality. Operating margins are improved by managing expenses, optimizing tax payments, streamlining financial reporting (and accentuating timeliness), and investing in new equipment. Financial leverage entails optimizing inventory and cash flow, improving the ability to access capital through enhanced liquidity, and improving key financial metrics. Finally, to bolster capability and sustainability, a company must close the gap in crucial management skills, decentralize organizational knowledge, and ensure an effective advisory board is in place.

The best succession plan, in short, entails ensuring the company is operating at peak performance. The goal is to give the enterprise a bright future—one that attracts new ownership, secures customer loyalty, and inspires the management team and employees to remain aboard and face new challenges and opportunities.

# ACKNOWLEDGMENTS

The Best Managed process has allowed us privileged access to senior executives, owners, founders, and employees of some of Canada's most outstanding enterprises. We owe the highest level of gratitude to the many business leaders who entrusted us with their insight and best practices.

*Power of the Best* is a unique composition of success stories from entrepreneurial business leaders across Canada. We are honoured to have had this rare glimpse inside Canada's most admired private companies.

Many thanks to the owners, management teams, employees, and families who have devoted countless hours to participate in the Best Managed program. By taking part in the program and this book, these companies have generously shared their business challenges and achievements, and thereby improved the program, their enterprises, and all Canadian businesses.

Thank you to the many members of the Best Managed team for their dedication and support of the program over twenty years and their assistance with this project.

Thank you to our esteemed program sponsors, CIBC, the *National Post*, and Queen's School of Business, which continue to contribute toward impactful events and thought leadership to the Best Managed community each year.

Also, thank you to our partners at Deloitte who asked us to lead their approach to this important business community.

Last but certainly not least, thank you to our families for your unwavering support. John and Peter serve many of Canada's best private companies, and this can be a demanding and time consuming venture that frequently takes us away from our families. Peter thanks his wife, Mary Ellen, and daughters Kalee and Eryn, while John thanks his wife, Julie, and daughters Alessia and Santina.

We dedicate this book to the Best Managed community, a network that has transformed the Canadian business landscape.

Peter Brown and John Hughes
Deloitte

## CONTRIBUTORS

Best Managed Companies
4ReFuel
Acadian Seaplants
All Weather Windows
Alliance Energy Group of
    Companies
Apex Distribution
Associate Veterinary Clinics
Bragg
Brock Solutions
Burnbrae
Cactus Club

Calco Environmental Group
CBI Health
Chaussures Régence
Concentra Financial
Conestoga Cold Storage
Deeley Harley-Davidson
DIRTT
Evans Consoles
Farm Boy
Floform
Fountain Tire
Friesens Corporation

Goodlife Fitness

Great Little Box

Great Western Brewing

Groupe Deschenes Inc

JV Driver

Knightsbridge

M. Sullivan and Son Limited.

Maple Reinders

Maritime Travel

Mayhew

McCain

Modern Niagara Group

Monarch Industries

Running Room Inc

Saskatchewan Minerals

Sirius Satellite Radio

Solutions 2 Go

SpinMaster

SteamWhistle

Supreme Steel

Vector Construction

Western Sales

Wheels

# INDEX